SUSAN M. WEINSCHENK, PH.D.

NEURO WEB DESIGN

what makes them click?

New Riders

VOICES THAT MATTER™

NEURO WEB DESIGN
SUSAN M. WEINSCHENK, PH.D.

New Riders
1249 Eighth Street
Berkeley, CA 94710
510/524-2178
510/524-2221 (fax)

Find us on the Web at: www.newriders.com
To report errors, please send a note to errata@peachpit.com

New Riders is an imprint of Peachpit, a division of Pearson Education.

PROJECT EDITOR: **Michael J. Nolan**
DEVELOPMENT EDITOR: **Jeff Riley**
PRODUCTION EDITOR: **Tracey Croom**
COPY EDITOR: **Marta Justak**
PROOFREADER: **Darren Meiss**
INDEXER: **Joy Dean Lee**
COVER DESIGN: **RHDG**
INTERIOR DESIGN: **Chrils Gillespie, Happenstance Type-O-Rama**

ISBN 13: 978-0-321-60360-9
ISBN 10: 0-321-60360-5

9 8 7 6 5

Printed and bound in the United States of America

NEURO WEB DESIGN

For my great family who gives me love and support: Peter, Maisie, and Guthrie.

ACKNOWLEDGEMENTS

I RECEIVED GREAT help and advice from the whole group at Peachpit Press, including Michael Nolan, who helped me form the idea of the book and shepherd it through Peachpit; and Jeff Riley, my development editor, whose sense of humor via email at midnight gave me the little bit more energy I needed during late-night editing sessions.

Thank you also to Guthrie Weinschenk and Maisie Weinschenk for their help with several photos that are in the book, and thank you to David Mitropoulos-Rundus for his unflagging encouragement and support.

ABOUT THE AUTHOR

DR. SUSAN WEINSCHENK has a Ph.D. in Psychology and a career since 1979 applying what we know about people to the design of technology. She is a speaker, teacher, mentor, and consultant to business clients worldwide. Susan writes a blog on Neuro Web Design at www.whatmakesthemclick. blogspot.com and maintains the www.neuroweb book.com Web site. She has two children and lives with her husband in Wisconsin.

CONTENTS

1

Designing Web Sites for Persuasion and the Unconscious Mind

ON A RECENT VACATION, you broke your digital camera. Now you have to buy a new one. You'd only had the old one for six months and hadn't even learned to use all the features. You liked the camera you had, but maybe there are better or cheaper ones now? Maybe you don't need all those features that you hadn't used in six months. You go online to check out cameras. Which Web site will you go to? Why did you choose that Web site? Will you go to more than one Web site? Will you buy it online after all? Which camera will you choose? How will you make that decision?

We think that we are reasonable, rational people and that our decisions are made by careful thinking. But the reality is that the Web site we pick, what we decide to do while there, and whether we buy or not are decisions and actions that we make in a largely unconscious way. Although some part of our decisions on which camera to buy, and where to buy it from, might come from the rational part of our brain, many of our decisions and actions are based on emotion, and many are based on automatic triggers that we react to from something we see on the Web site. Some (even most) of our actions are initiated from parts of our brain that we don't have conscious access to. Many of our decisions, reactions, and behaviors are governed by mental processes of which we are not even aware.

Over the past 100 years, neuroscientists and neuropsychologists have been studying the human brain to understand how it works and why we do the things we do. And over the past 10 years, new technologies of brain scanning have allowed these researchers to verify what their previous research had hinted at. There are now answers to these questions: What are the parts of the brain that govern our behavior? Which parts of our brain will be active when we make our decision about the camera?

The brain is complex, and I'm not going to attempt to teach you all about brain science in this book. But I am going to explain some of what neuroscientists know about the brain, connect that knowledge to our everyday behavior, and connect it especially to our everyday behavior on the Internet.

> *Your Web experiences are highly influenced by unconscious thoughts and actions that are controlled by various parts of your brain.*

YOU'RE SO SMART YOU HAVE THREE BRAINS

WE OFTEN TALK about the human brain as if it were one large amorphous part of our body, but there are distinct parts of the brain that have distinct functions. In this book I'm going to simplify it all by referring to three different brains:

- The old brain
- The mid brain
- The new brain

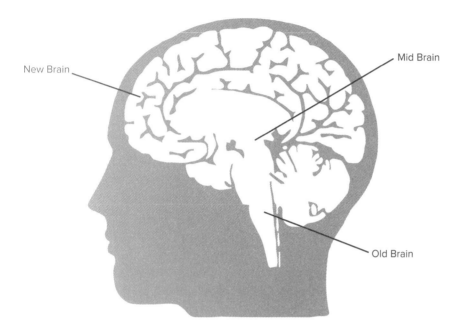

The old brain gets its name from the idea that it developed first in the evolutionary history of animals. The old brain is concerned with our survival. The old brain is constantly looking at the environment around us, deciding what is safe and what isn't. It's also the part of our brain that takes care of things automatically, such as digestion, movement, and breathing.

The mid brain is where emotions are processed. It's what causes you to feel things, and it's the root of a lot of your impulse buying.

The new brain, or cortex, is the most recent structure identified (from an evolutionary standpoint). Language processing, speech, reading, playing music, listening to music, thinking thoughts, planning—these are all done with the new brain. It's your new brain that is reading this book.

Much of the processing of the old and mid brain occurs outside of our conscious awareness. The part of our brain processing that we are aware of happens in the new brain.

WHAT REALLY MAKES US DIFFERENT FROM ANIMALS?

THE GENERAL OPINION among brain scholars is that it is our cortex, or new brain, that distinguishes us as humans, particularly the part of the cortex called the **pre-frontal cortex**. This is the part of the brain where reasoning and logical thought comes from, and it seems to be the most recent from an evolutionary point of view. Many scientists think that this pre-frontal cortex is especially what makes us human.

It is certainly true that humans have a pre-frontal cortex and most other animals don't. And it is also true that "higher" mammals have a cortex and "lower" animals don't. But it is even more accurate to say that what makes us human is that we have a pre-frontal cortex that *interacts* with other parts of our brain. What really makes us human is that in addition to the new brain cortex, we have a mid brain where emotions are generated and interpreted, and we have an old brain that watches out for our very survival. What really makes us human is that we have all three. And all three work together. Here's an example.

www.flickr.com/photos/kylemay

You are driving in your car (old brain is moving muscles, scanning the road, new brain is processing visual data and talking to the old brain so that you stay between the lines), and you are thinking about an argument you had with your brother over the weekend (new brain is remembering the argument, mid brain is reliving the argument emotionally). You are, after the fact, thinking about the things you should have said, but didn't. You feel upset that you didn't defend yourself (mid brain feeling upset, new brain thinking about things to say, old brain still driving the car).

Suddenly, a car in front of you brakes (old brain notices that something has changed that needs attention, old brain floods system with hormones to heighten your ability to fight or flee, old brain has you slam on brakes, mid brain feels scared that you almost had an accident and relieved that you didn't, new brain analyzes situation and thinks about what you might have done differently).

While you drive the rest of the way home, you relive the near miss (new brain plays the memory over and over, mid brain feels the emotions again). You decide not to be angry with your brother any more, life is too short (mid brain feels forgiving and happy, new brain makes decision to call brother on phone, but decides to wait until you get home since talking on a cell phone while driving may not be a good idea right now, old brain is still driving the car).

Our physical bodies and the parts of the brain that govern them are inextricably linked with the parts of our brain that regulate emotions and the parts of the brain that deal with conscious thought and reasoning. These are separate systems in the brain, but they all work together. Our feelings and our reasoning are affected by our physical movement. It is our old brain that is regulating digestion and sleep, but there are controls in the mid brain that govern our emotions and feelings and can then affect our digestion and sleep. And what we think of as our "mind" (the new brain) has an effect on emotions, feelings, and digestion and sleep, too. Although we have three different brain systems, they are all connected and interrelated.

We've inherited a mindset that tells us that the mind and body are separate, but the research and data show us they are not. Antonio Damasio (1994) calls this separation of mind and body "Descartes' Error."

For more information about Descartes' Error, see http://en. wikipedia.org/wiki/Descartes'_Error

WHAT HAPPENS WHEN WE FEEL AN EMOTION ANYWAY?

www.flickr.com/megyarsh

YOUR PHONE RINGS, and you pick it up to find that a good friend of yours is in the hospital with a serious illness. There will be a series of events that will happen in your body and in your brain automatically, and eventually you will become aware that you have a feeling, perhaps of sadness. You remember the last time you saw your friend, and you recall the trip you made together. If we could hook you up to some machines to measure activity in your brain and your body, we would see that the old brain is activated, as well as two parts of your mid brain called the **amygdala**.

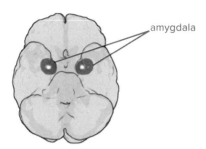

amygdala

Each amygdala is about the size and shape of an almond, and they collectively play a very important role in this book. They are the parts of the brain that regulate emotions. In addition to seeing your amygdala light up, we might be able to see activity in your visual cortex when you were remembering that last trip, measure that your heart is racing, and even determine that your immune system is depressed. You may start to cry. Your amygdala is probably governing this reaction, but there is activity in all three parts of your brain.

THERE'S A LOT GOING ON UP THERE THAT WE DON'T EVEN KNOW ABOUT

WHAT MAKES US human is that we have all three brains. But since the new brain is the only part of brain functioning that we are conscious of, we think it is the most important player. Our mid brain (emotions) and old brain (automatic functioning) processing are, for the most part, unconscious, but here's the interesting thing: our behavior and our decision-making is just as affected, actually, even *more* affected by our old brain and our mid brain than it is by our new brain.

What does this mean? It means that we think we make decisions about how to act and what to do consciously, but actually most of our decision-making and behavior is governed by unconscious processing. We can't really separate what we do consciously from the unconscious aspects.

HEY, I'M IN CONSCIOUS CONTROL OF HOW I ACT, RIGHT?

IT CAN BE disturbing to think that we might not be in conscious control of our thoughts, emotions, or actions. There is actually a lot of research that shows that we are not in conscious control of a lot of our behavior.

In 1996, John Bargh ran a series of experiments where participants were provided with word lists to unscramble. They unscrambled word sentences to form grammatically correct sentences. For example, they were provided with five words—*he it finds hides instantly*—and were asked to unscramble and use four of the words to make a grammatically correct sentence (such as *He finds it instantly.*)

There were three conditions in the experiment:

- In the **Rude Condition**, many of the words in the unscrambled sentences were rude (for example, words like *aggressively*, *bold*, *rude*, *disturb*, and *intrude*).

- In the **Polite Condition**, many of the words were polite (such as *respect*, *honor*, *appreciate*, and *patiently*).

- In the **Neutral Condition**, the words were neither polite nor rude.

After the participants completed the word-scrambling task, they were instructed to walk down the hall to find the experimenter and tell him they were done. The experimenter was at the end of the hall, his back to the participants, pretending to be giving instructions to another participant (who was actually part of the experiment). The researchers measured whether participants would stand and wait for the experimenter to finish his instructions, or if they would interrupt.

Would those people who had unscrambled the rude words act any differently than the people who unscrambled the polite words?

Fewer than 20 percent of the participants in the Polite Condition interrupted within 10 minutes. Almost 40 percent of the participants in the Neutral Condition interrupted within 10 minutes. More than 60 percent of the rude group interrupted within 10 minutes.

Later, when asked if they thought the unscrambling word task had any influence on their behavior, all participants said no.

Our actions can be affected by things that we are not aware of.

We are often unaware of the reasons for our own behavior.

HAVE YOU HAD A BRILLIANT UNCONSCIOUS THOUGHT LATELY?

THE NEW FRONTIER of thought is actually the unconscious. The latest idea is that we are processing information and "thinking" unconsciously all the time. This is why when we are trying to solve a problem and we stop working on it and go to lunch, the solution will suddenly appear as we are munching on our sandwich or driving in the car back to work. Your unconscious was working on the problem, but you weren't aware of it.

Wilson (2002) defines the unconscious as "mental processes that are inaccessible to the conscious mind, but influence judgments, feelings or behavior...shortcuts that size up our environment, interpret and initiate behavior quickly."

Because the unconscious is, well, unconscious, we don't appreciate all it does. Imagine a day without the unconscious. We wouldn't be able to get through five minutes. The estimate from neuroscientists is that our five senses are taking in 11 million pieces of information every second. And how many of those are we processing consciously? A mere 40! So we need the unconscious to deal with the other 10,999,960 pieces of information each second, or we would be overwhelmed in a matter of seconds. Our unconscious mind lets us process all the incoming data from our environment, and it instantly decides whether it is good or bad, something to avoid and run away from, or something to run toward. Our unconscious is a huge efficient shortcut tool, showing us what to pay attention to consciously.

"Automatic cognitive processes are internal automatons that help us navigate a multifaceted and complex environment by slicing it into easily digestible bites. They...can thus free our very limited-capacity consciousness from many burdens."
Ran R. Hassin (Hassin, 2005)

YOUR UNCONSCIOUS IS SMARTER AND FASTER THAN YOUR CONSCIOUS MIND

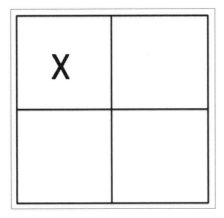

YOU'RE SITTING IN front of a computer screen that is divided into four quadrants. The experimenter tells you to watch for an X that is going to appear in one of the quadrants and to press one of the four buttons in front of you to in-dicate which quadrant the X is in. This experiment was performed by Lewicki in 1988.

The participants didn't know it, but there was a complex rule about where the X would appear. For example, the X never appeared in the same square two times in a row; the location of the third X was dependent upon the location of the second. The location of the fourth X was dependent upon the location of the set of Xs for the previous two trials. Lastly, an X never appeared in a spot unless it had appeared in at least two of the other squares.

Whew! The rules were complicated, but participants learned them. That was evident since as they continued, their performance steadily improved—they got faster and faster at pressing the correct buttons.

But not one of the participants could articulate what the rules were. Nor were they aware they were learning rules. Yet their performance improved. Their unconscious mind was learning the rules for them and guiding their behavior about which button to press.

Just when participants were starting to perform well, the rules suddenly changed. The participants then started making mistakes, and their re-sponse times increased. They noticed that they weren't doing well, but they didn't know why. They had no awareness that there were rules that no longer worked. Interestingly, they consciously looked for reasons as to why their performance had deteriorated. They said things like they had "lost the rhythm" or that the experimenters were flashing subliminal pictures on the screen to distract them (which wasn't true).

> *We often don't know why we do the things we do. But we are quick to make up a reason that we actually believe, even though it's not true. Psychologists call this* **confabulation.**

Our unconscious minds are very smart. But we don't control them.

BUT WE KNOW WHAT WE LIKE
AND WHAT WE DON'T, RIGHT?

FOR MANY YEARS I would camp with my family every summer. I liked camping—getting out in nature, being with my family, and getting away from it all. I

thought of myself as an outdoors kind of person. But every time I started getting ready for camping, I would become anxious, irritable, and very unhappy. The truth was that I didn't like camping at all. I didn't like sleeping on the ground, and I was nervous about taking two small children out in the wilderness in a canoe.

We don't always know what we like. We are often not aware of our feelings. Our feelings and emotions originate in the amygdala in the mid brain. So we can have one set of feelings there, but actually think we have another set of feelings in our new brain.

www.flickr.com/photos/photomonkey

SO THEN, WHAT MAKES US CLICK?

MOST OWNERS OF Web sites have their Web sites for a reason. There are target behaviors that they want us to engage in—quite often, even several target behaviors. An e-commerce site wants us to choose products and buy them. A non-profit site wants us to loan money to help small business owners in different parts of the world. A Fortune 1000 company wants us to be impressed with what they do and buy more stock in the company. A site based on ad revenue wants us to come to the site and then click on an ad. A site that is trying to get acquired wants us to come to the site and register to be a member so that the company can say they have x million registered members. Almost all Web sites have target behaviors. How do they get us to engage in the target behavior? How do they get us to buy, register, donate, and click? What makes us click?

To get us to click, they have to persuade us. But don't make the mistake of thinking that the best way to persuade us is to make a logical presentation. Most behavior and decision-making isn't conscious. That means that they will have to engage the mid brain and the old brain, in addition to the new brain. We want to think that we are making logical decisions, even though we aren't. The most effective Web sites are Web sites that talk to all three brains. When the Web site engages all three brains, then we click.

And that is what this book is about. We'll survey the science on persuasion and apply it to the design of Web sites to see why some Web sites are so effective and others aren't. Fortunately, there is a lot of science around this; it's just that it hasn't yet been applied to the design of sites.

And that's why you are reading this book.

When you are done, you'll know what that camera Web site could do to grab your attention: how it could talk to your old brain, your mid brain, and your new brain—and thereby make you click

---

We like to think we make our decisions based on careful thought, but most of our decisions and actions come from our unconscious.

The unconscious is smart, efficient, and fast. We couldn't survive without it.

BOTTOM LINE

Web sites that "speak" to all three brains (old brain, mid brain, new brain) are the most effective.

2

Wanting to Belong:
The Power of Social Validation

HAVE YOU EVER attended a church or religious service that was not one that you were used to? It might have gone something like this. You weren't sure what was going to happen next. People were responding or praying or singing or chanting in what seemed like a foreign language. They seemed to be sitting, or standing, or kneeling at various cues. You surreptitiously stole glances at everyone around you and tried to imitate what they were doing. If everyone stood up and put a paper bag on their heads and turned around three times, you probably would have looked to see where your paper bag was.

Why is the behavior of others so compelling? Why do we pay attention to and copy what others do? It's called **social validation**.

Most people view themselves as independent thinkers, meaning that they like to think they are unique individuals. The truth is, however, that the need to fit in and belong is wired into our brains and our biology. We want to fit in. We want to be like the crowd. This is such a strong drive, that when people are in a social situation, they will look to others to see how to behave. It's not a conscious process; we don't know we're doing it.

The need to fit and belong is wired into our brains and our biology.

THE (NOT QUITE TRUE) TRAGEDY OF KITTY GENOVESE

ONE NIGHT IN 1964 a young woman by the name of Kitty Genovese was attacked in Queens, NY and stabbed to death. According to an article in *The New York Times*, she was stabbed multiple times by the same man over a 30-minute period, screamed for help repeatedly during the attacks, and yet no one went to her aid. The article said that 38 people witnessed the attack, but no one intervened to help.

The New York Times article started a storm of speculation by social scientists about why normal, upstanding citizens would let something like that happen. Why did no one go to Kitty's aid? Is it because people are apathetic? Are they afraid that if they intervene they'll be killed too? A line of research into what is called the **bystander effect** was started.

Latane and Darley (1970) conducted a series of studies culminating in a book in 1970 called *The Unresponsive Bystander: Why Doesn't He Help?*

In one of Latane and Darley's studies, they would have someone act as though they were having an epileptic seizure on a city street. Would someone coming upon the person in distress stop and help? They studied varying numbers of onlookers. If a single bystander came upon the person in distress, that individual helped 85 percent of the time. If five people were present, they found that one person stepped forward to help only 31 percent of the time. This research supported the notion that if there were others around in a particular situation, most individuals seemed to look to everyone else in the group to determine how they should behave. Most of the time, no one took action. They essentially stood around and looked for somebody else to act.

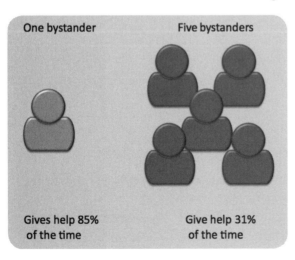

One bystander

Five bystanders

Gives help 85% of the time

Give help 31% of the time

In another Latane and Darley study (1968), participants sat in a room and completed questionnaires. While they completed their paperwork, smoke was released into the room from a vent. The experimental conditions varied:

- In one experimental condition, there was only one subject in the room, and that subject was not aware of the study.

- In another, there were three individuals in the room, but two were aware of the experiment. Those two were instructed to act unconcerned and continue to fill out their questionnaires while smoke filled the room.

- In a third experimental condition, there were three subjects in the room, all of whom were entirely unaware of the experiment.

So what did people do? Did anyone take action by leaving the room and reporting the smoke?

In the first condition, 75 percent of the subjects left the room and reported the smoke. In the second condition, only 10 percent of the subjects left the room and reported the smoke. In the third experiment, 38 percent left the room and reported the smoke.

This research supports the notion that we look to others to validate what our behavior should be. The research shows that this is especially true when we're uncertain about what to do.

> *People look to others to decide what they should do. This is especially true when they are uncertain about whether or what action to take.*

The part about Kitty that is not quite true

A 1995 *New York Times* article cast doubt on the first article's description of the Kitty Genovese incident. The article raised the possibility that the number of people actually witnessing the event was exaggerated. Based on a later analysis of the data and the crime scene, it is likely that *some* people (but not necessarily *38* people) heard or saw something, and also noted that those individuals might have had difficulty figuring out what was going on. Still, the line of research that was started in the bystander effect is strong, and the data holds.

THE BYSTANDER EFFECT FOR GETTING HELP ONLINE

IN A MORE recent study on the bystander effect (Markey, 2000), Markey asked whether the bystander effect would work in chat groups.

- If you asked a question in a chat group, would your sex determine how long it would take to get an answer?

- Would the number of other people (bystanders) in the chat room affect the time it would take to get help?

- Finally, if you asked for help from a specific person and addressed him by name, would you receive help faster?

The results? Gender didn't have an effect, but the more people who were present in the chat group, the longer it took for someone to get help. Each additional person added to the chat group added about three seconds to the time it took to get help.

For example, with only two people in the chat room, it took 30 seconds to get a response. With 19 people in the chat room, it took over 65 seconds to get a response. If you addressed a particular person, then it was as though no one else were in the room, and it took only 30 seconds to get a response.

WHY WOULD YOU LISTEN TO TOTAL STRANGERS?

Imagine you're at a chain superstore looking for an HD flat-screen television. You stand there and stare at the large wall of HD televisions showing NASCAR races. An innocent bystander meanders by and you grab him and say,

"What do you think of this TV? Did you buy one? Would you buy it again if you had to do it all over?" He tells you his opinion and walks away. You grab the next person you see and say, "Hey there, do you have this TV? What do you think of it?" She tells you her opinion and walks away. You are at the store for 13 hours gathering opinions. This goes on until you feel secure in a decision.

Sound absurd? In the "real world," it is absurd. Online, it's not so absurd. However, you won't need 13 hours to browse products on a Web site. The online version of consumer feedback is faster. You can gather data by reading ratings and reviews. We will avidly read reviews from total strangers, and these reviews will sway our decision on whether, what, and when to buy. Why? We don't know who the people reviewing the product are, where they come from, their likes and dislikes, or if they are anything like us—and yet, we trust them. If we see that a product has received only one out of five stars, we don't even take a closer look. It's social validation at work.

What do others think?

How does social validation affect how we use Web sites? Online ratings and reviews influence us greatly—most powerfully at a non-conscious level.

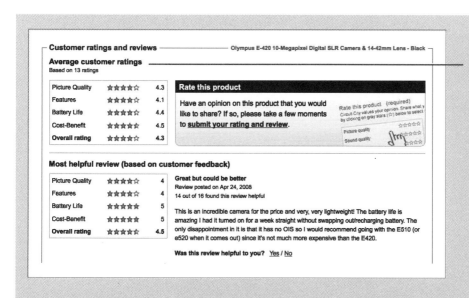

Ratings and reviews are the online equivalent of surveying a bunch of strangers in your favorite retail store.

There are lots of ways to use ratings. Some are more effective than others.

For example, the site that follows doesn't put any rating information on the first page. We have to click on a specific product before the rating appears. This means they aren't using social validation as effectively as they could.

By waiting until a later screen to show rating information, they risk losing our attention. We may never get to the next screen to even see the ratings.

There are no ratings or reviews at the first product page. They have ratings and reviews later, but they miss an opportunity up front.

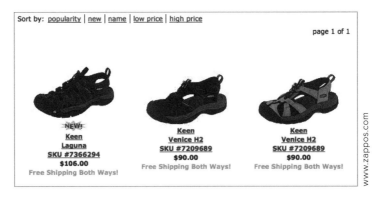

Once they show ratings, they do a great job. Notice they even have ratings on different criteria, such as comfort and look. They also show the number of reviewers. The more reviewers there are, the more powerful the impact of social validation will be.

Wow, 499 reviewers! They even have different categories of ratings.

And, finally, the actual reviews themselves.

Customer Rating/Review

Keen Venice H2
Number of reviews: 499
Average customer ratings:
Overall: ★★★★★ **Comfort:** ★★★★★ **Look:** ★★★★★

2008-07-17 11:31:09 Keen Venice H2
Reviewer: **Angelfish**
Overall: ★★★★★ **Comfort:** ★★★★★ **Look:** ★★★★☆
Shoe Size: Felt true to size
Shoe Width: Felt true to width
Shoe Arch: Excellent arch support

Great walking sandal - I've had my Venice H2's for a month now and just love them. I walked three miles in them the first day without any rubbing. They are great for long city walks...extremely comfortable and much nicer looking and cooler than sneakers and socks. Washable too. They ran true to size for me.

www.zappos.com

RECENT RESEARCH ON WEB SITE RECOMMENDATIONS FOR PRODUCTS VERSUS "EXPERIENCES"

De Vries and Pruyn (2007) studied whether recommendations influenced Web site visitors' decisions when buying digital cameras (**Product Condition**) and choosing tourist destinations (**Experiences Condition**). The researchers were interested in whether recommendations would be equally influential for both products and experiences. When recommendations were provided for a particular item, that item sold 20 percent more volume than an item for which there were no recommendations. If recommendations were provided for a particular travel destination, that destination was selected 10 percent more often than a destination for which there was no recommendation. If a photo of the person accompanied the travel recommendation, the travel experience condition increased to 20 percent.

What did others do?

Another effective variation is to show what other people actually ended up buying.

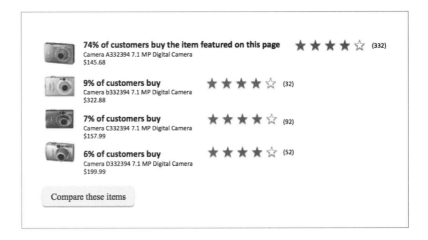

When the conscious mind kicks in

There is one way the conscious mind might kick in to the conversation. Sometimes (but it's rare), we start to get suspicious. This usually happens only if we have information that leads us to doubt ratings. For example, a friend of mine used to work at a company that hired people to post positive product ratings. "What if they're all fake?" she asked.

Now her cortex (**new brain**) is disagreeing with her old brain. Her **old brain** says, "I want to be like everyone else," even when she's not aware it's saying that. But her new brain says, "Maybe this isn't accurate data." The old brain will probably win in the end. If she reads some reviews that are not 100 percent positive, and if the people writing those reviews seem like a "real" person who actually used the product, then the new brain's objections can be squelched fairly easily.

"Listen to others? Not me, I'm logical"

Ratings and reviews work unconsciously to activate our need for social validation. But they also give us the rationalization we need or want after we have made our decision unconsciously. Data, charts, graphs, and statistics allow us to tell ourselves we are making the wise choice.

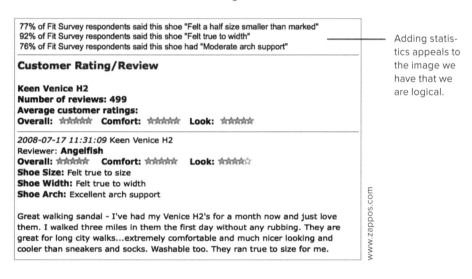

> 77% of Fit Survey respondents said this shoe "Felt a half size smaller than marked"
> 92% of Fit Survey respondents said this shoe "Felt true to width"
> 76% of Fit Survey respondents said this shoe had "Moderate arch support"
>
> **Customer Rating/Review**
>
> **Keen Venice H2**
> **Number of reviews: 499**
> **Average customer ratings:**
> **Overall:** ★★★★★ **Comfort:** ★★★★★ **Look:** ★★★★★
>
> *2008-07-17 11:31:09 Keen Venice H2*
> Reviewer: **Angelfish**
> **Overall:** ★★★★★ **Comfort:** ★★★★★ **Look:** ★★★★☆
> **Shoe Size:** Felt true to size
> **Shoe Width:** Felt true to width
> **Shoe Arch:** Excellent arch support
>
> Great walking sandal - I've had my Venice H2's for a month now and just love them. I walked three miles in them the first day without any rubbing. They are great for long city walks...extremely comfortable and much nicer looking and cooler than sneakers and socks. Washable too. They ran true to size for me.

Adding statistics appeals to the image we have that we are logical.

www.zappos.com

Statistics and a bar chart appeal to our idea that we are making a logical choice, even though our choice is based on unconscious processing.

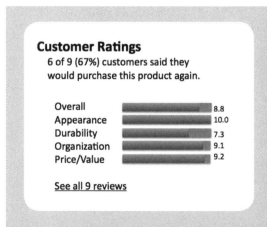

Customer Ratings
6 of 9 (67%) customers said they would purchase this product again.

Overall	�	8.8
Appearance		10.0
Durability		7.3
Organization		9.1
Price/Value		9.2

See all 9 reviews

Not only statistics, but a bar chart too. Even more logical!

Tell me a story

The most powerful ratings and reviews involve narratives and storytelling. See Chapter 10 for more information about the power of stories.

At this next site, they provide information about the person who wrote the review, as well as a summary of that individual's experience with the product. They have sketched out a mini "persona" and "scenario." This adds to the narrative element, making the review even more powerful.

> *Ideally, the information provided about reviewers is more detailed than the name and location you see here. You'll learn more about that later in this chapter.*

The 'persona' tells us about the person and what they used the product for. On the left are stories.

 Date posted: September 18
Reviewed by: Lisa, San Francisco

"I bought this stroller when I found out that I was pregnant with TWINS! What a surprise that was! All of a sudden I had to be super frugal with my money, AND had to plan for two of everything. This stroller was super easy to put together, came to me in less than 2 days, and is even kind of pretty. It is very low maintenance, easy on all fronts, and was everything I expected. The babies on the other hand....."

•Type of user: Mom
•Frequency of use: Every day
•Occupation: Stay at Home Mom
•Gender: Female

 Date posted: September 5
Reviewed by: Bob, Los Angeles

"I took up jogging when after my son was born as a way to have some alone time. Now that he's a little bit older, he loves to come with me. This jogger makes our outings so much fun for both of us. The shocks are great, the steering column works well, it has a great emergency break. I love this product so very much!"

•Type of user: Athlete/Dad
•Frequency of use: Three times a week
•Occupation: Financial Planner
•Gender: Male

Customer feedback is not limited to the product itself. Reviewers can post comments regarding the company.

Customer Testimonials

" Zappos is the best!!! This is our third time ordering shoes from Zappos and they have been nothing but excellent. We ordered shoes for my daughter and the next day they were at my doorstep. This saves me time and gas! Thanks Zappos for being so loyal to your customers. "

~ Lisa Q, 2008-07-22

www.zappos.com

Reviews of the company as a whole are effective too.

But who are they?

Reviewer feedback is most powerful when we know more about the reviewers than just their names and the dates their feedback was posted.

We listen more closely to people we know and trust. If we are listening to someone we don't know, then we will try to (unconsciously) determine if the person is like us (for more information about this concept, see Chapter 8). We are also very influenced by stories, which you'll learn more about in Chapter 10.

Taking this into account, what kinds of ratings and reviews will influence us the most? We're most influenced (in this order) when:

1 We are most influenced when we know the person and the person is telling a story. It is unlikely that we will be reading a review online by someone we actually know. That brings us then to #2.

2 We are somewhat less influenced when we don't necessarily know the person, but it's still someone we can imagine because there is a persona, a name (or company name). Again, it always helps if the person is telling a story.

3 We're even less influenced when we don't know the person, and we can't imagine them, but we are provided with a story.

4 We are least influenced when we don't know the person, and we're provided with only a rating.

In the example that follows, we're at least provided with the full name of the person and her company.

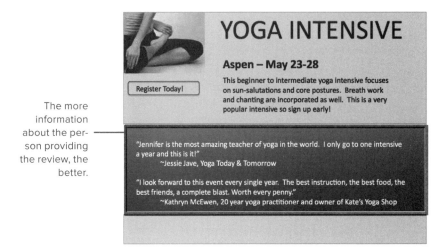

The more information about the person providing the review, the better.

What are you watching?

Social validation not only influences our purchase decisions, but it also affects other behavior, such as how we might experience a Web site. For example, a highly-rated video might influence us to watch the video ourselves, thereby influencing our behavior. Here are ratings on videos to watch at YouTube.

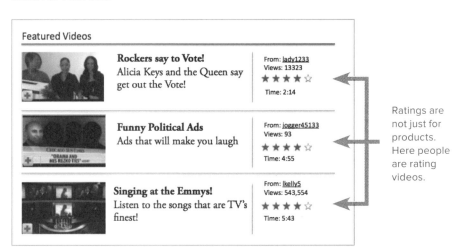

Ratings are not just for products. Here people are rating videos.

Showing how many people performed a particular action at the Web site is powerful. This example shows how many people watched a particular video.

Theo Jansen - Kinetic Sculptor

0:33 / 1:05

Rate: ★ ★ ★ ★ ☆   445 ratings   Views: **399,994**

This video has been watched by a lot of people.

And here's an interesting twist: What are others doing right now at the same Web site?

Videos being watched right now...

01:13   02:15   01:05   00:30   03:23

Even better, show me what people are doing RIGHT NOW.

We're called to act when we know what others have experienced with a product, or we know what they're doing at a Web site, or we even know what they are doing *right now*.

We will do what others are doing. We will be drawn to belong.

BOTTOM LINE

3

Feeling Indebted: How to Build in Reciprocity and Concession

EVERY YEAR at holiday time I agonize whether or not to send a holiday gift to Deidre. She's been sending me the same box of cheese for 20 years. She lives in California. I live in Wisconsin. I'm surrounded by cheese. The last thing I need is a box of cheese. Often the box of cheese she sends is from a company in Wisconsin, which is ironic. Even more ironic is the fact that I started this chain of gift-giving. Deidre and I started off as business associates and then got to know each other as friends. One year I got caught up in the "spirit of the season" and sent her a holiday present in the mail. Shortly thereafter the first box of cheese showed up. The following year the box of cheese arrived early, and I had to send her a present in return. On and on the gift-giving has continued for 20 years. I sometimes think that I should stop sending a present. Then maybe she wouldn't send me the cheese, and we could stop this worn-out holiday tradition. But would she think badly of me if one year I didn't send a gift? And so the tradition continues. Maybe Deidre will read this book and get mad at me and stop the cheese!

A SENSE OF OBLIGATION

WE RETURN FAVORS and exchange gifts. Sometimes we do this out of love or for fun. But many times we give gifts or favors out of a sense of obligation. If I give you a gift or do you a favor, you will feel indebted to me. You will want to give me a gift or do me a favor in return; possibly to be nice, but mainly to get rid of the feeling of indebtedness. This is a largely unconscious feeling, and it is quite strong. This is called **reciprocity**.

The theory is that this gift-giving and favor-swapping developed in human societies because it is useful in the survival of the species. If one person gives someone something (food, shelter, money, a gift, or favor), that person will trigger the indebtedness. If the person who did the gifting finds him or herself in need of something in the future, he can "call-in" the favor. These "deals" or arrangements encouraged cooperation between individuals in a group, and that cooperation allowed the group to grow and support each other.

> *Richard Leakey, a paleontologist and son of the famous archeologists Louis and Mary Leakey, wrote "We are human because our ancestors learned to share their food and their skills in an honored network of obligation." (Leakey and Lewin, 1978)*

HOW BIG SHOULD IT BE?

RECIPROCITY DOESN'T MEAN that if we give others a gift we will automatically get a gift in return. What does happen is that if we give them a gift, we will trigger a feeling of indebtedness —a feeling of indebtedness that they'll want to get rid of by responding with gifts or favors. Sometimes they will ignore their feelings, but those feelings *will* linger. It might even take a long time for them to act on the feelings. Another interesting aspect about reciprocity: when they return the gift or favor, that gift or favor may be different in value than the original gift. Usually, they won't reciprocate with something of lesser value—that would leave them with a feeling of an unpaid debt. Often, they reciprocate with something of higher value than the original gift.

SENDING CHRISTMAS CARDS TO STRANGERS—AND HOW ABOUT $5 CANS OF SODA?

IN A RESEARCH study by Kunz and Wolcott (1976), researchers sent out Christmas cards to random people and received cards back from many of them—all strangers! Like my situation with Deidre, many of these Christmas cards kept arriving year after year.

Imagine that you've signed up to participate in a research study on creativity. You go into a room with another participant, whom we'll call Joe. The two of you are in the room working separately on your creativity tasks. After a while, the experimenter comes in the room to tell you that you'll have a 10-minute break. Joe asks if he can leave the room during the break, and the experimenter says yes. Joe comes back a few minutes later with two cans of soda. He's opened one, but he hands the other one to you and says, "I asked the guy if it was okay to bring a soda in here and he said yes, so I brought one for you, too." You thank him and open the soda. The experimenter comes in the room and starts the art creativity tasks again. Another short while later the experimenter says that he has to first check on something, then you are free to go. While he is gone, Joe says to you, "Hey, would you be interested in buying some raffle tickets? The person who sells the most tickets gets a prize." You say okay and buy three raffle tickets for $5.

It turns out that Joe is really part of the experiment. The experiment was on reciprocity. If Joe gave you a can of soda, would you then reciprocate and buy the raffle tickets when he asked you? Half of the time, Joe offers a soda. The other half, he doesn't. The results? When Joe brings you a soda, you're twice as likely to purchase a raffle ticket than when Joe *doesn't* bring you a soda. You feel that you have to buy the raffle tickets because he gave you a gift—even though the raffle tickets cost a lot more than the soda did (Regan, 1971).

The power of reciprocity has been well known to people who manage direct marketing campaigns.

For example, a mailing that solicited donations for a veterans group generated an average response rate of 18 percent. When the mailing campaign included personalized address labels, the donations almost doubled to 35 percent (Cialdini, 2007). And it seems that the principle of reciprocity occurs across most, if not all, cultures (Heinrich et al, 2001).

> *In a mail appeal for donations, the normal response rate was 18 percent. If, however, the mailing included personalized address labels, the donations almost doubled to 35 percent.*

Reciprocity is used to persuade you to perform some action, such as making a purchase, volunteering, or funding a project.

WHEN ACCEPTING NO FOR AN ANSWER IS ACTUALLY A GIFT

LET'S SAY THAT you are on the local school board and I'm part of a group of parents that would like to get new playground equipment. We've heard that there are some extra funds left over this year in the school budget. The parent group has selected me to approach the school board and ask for $5,000 of the fund balance for the playground equipment project.

At the meeting in which I'm making my request, I shock the rest of the parent group by asking for $7,500, not $5,000. You and the rest of the school board shake your heads and say, "No, no, we can't possibly spend that much money for playground equipment." I look disappointed and then say, "Oh, well, we do have a reduced plan for $5,000." You ask to see the reduced plan, and I walk out of the meeting with the $5,000 project approved.

What just happened is called **concession**. When you said no to me, and I accepted that no, my no acted as a gift to you. As a result, you were indebted to me. You had to reciprocate with something. So when I offered the reduced plan for $5,000, you said yes as a way to relieve the indebtedness.

This tactic is sometimes called "**rejection then retreat**." The initiator asks a favor that is well above what most people would agree to. After the refusal, the initiator then asks for another favor that is more reasonable and received exactly what he or she wanted in the first place.

CONCESSION BUILDS COMMITMENT, TOO

WHAT IF I stopped you on the street one day and asked you to chaperone a group of troubled youth on a one-day trip to the zoo? Cialdini et.al. (1975) did just that. If you were like most people in his study, you said no. Only 17 percent of people said yes.

If he first asked people to spend two hours a week as a counselor for the youth for a minimum of two years (a larger request), every one of them declined—100 percent refusal. If he *then* asked them to chaperone a group of troubled youth on a one-day trip to the zoo, 50 percent agreed. That is nearly three times the number of those who agreed when they were only asked to chaperone. That's concession working.

That's how many people agreed to chaperone. But how many actually showed up? Eighty-five percent of the people in the concession group actually showed up, compared with only 50 percent of the group that did not go through the concession process.

A similar study by the same group also found that the concession technique resulted in a higher likelihood that people would volunteer again (84 percent vs. 43 percent). Concession resulted in a greater number of those willing to commit.

For concession to have an effect, the first offer has to be beyond what people will normally agree to, but still has to be considered reasonable. If the first offer is totally outlandish, the retreat (second) request won't work. In addition, the retreat offer has to be seen as "fair."

> *Ask for more than what you really want and then offer a concession to a lesser request (which is what you really wanted).*

GIVING THINGS AWAY AT A WEB SITE

ANYTIME SOMETHING IS given away at a Web site, it has created an opportunity to build indebtedness and reciprocity. This is perhaps a little more complex and subtle than it seems.

Let's say there is an e-commerce site offering free shipping on orders over $75. Is this reciprocity?

Consider the fact that we not only have to buy something, we have to spend a certain amount of money—perhaps more than we were willing to spend. By agreeing to spend more than we'd originally planned, we presented the first gift (our willingness to spend more money). The company then reciprocates by giving us free shipping. This feels like an even exchange, at best—as such, the offer for free shipping will *not* create a feeling of indebtedness in us.

Free shipping with conditions, may not be seen as a gift and therefore may not trigger reciprocity.

Give a gift to someone special. Save a lot.   FREE Shipping on orders of $75.00 or more>

For us to consider free shipping to be the gift, we have to feel as if the offer has no strings attached. At Zappos.com's online shoe store, they offer free shipping with no strings attached. Even better, they offer free shipping if you decide to return the shoes. Now that's special, which makes the offer feel like a gift to us when we shop their online store.

Zappos.com has free shipping, no strings attached AND free shipping if you want to return what you bought.

Free gifts are very powerful. If a site gives us free gifts, no strings attached—that will trigger reciprocity.

Several years ago, Lands End (a clothing company in the United States) sent me a small Christmas tree ornament with a card. The card read, "Just to say thanks for being our customer." No coupons, nothing else, just a little ornament and the card. That small gesture 15 years ago continues to influence my behavior today. Every time I need to buy an article of clothing that I could buy from LL Bean, or Eddie Bauer, or any number of places, I always stop and think, "I should see if Lands End has what I am looking for first."

So, giving a gift away at a Web site that has no strings attached could procure a customer or friend for a long time.

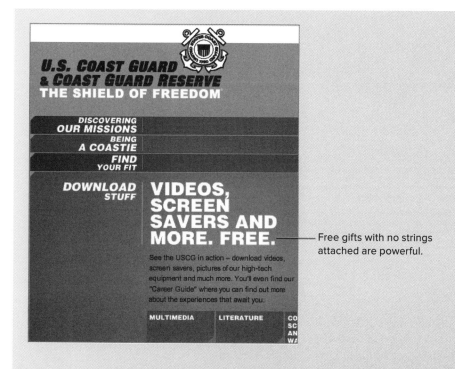

Free gifts with no strings attached are powerful.

GIVE AWAY FREE INFO

ONE WAY THAT Web sites give gifts is by giving the gift of useful information. For example, if an e-commerce site sells cameras, there could be a portion of the site that features an excellent guide to taking pictures. If users come to the site to read about taking pictures, and they appreciate the information that is provided for free, they might feel as if they've been given a gift. This doesn't guarantee that they'll buy a camera from the site, but it greatly increases the chances that they will—and that might just keep them from visiting your competitor's site. Even if they do not purchase right away, they are likely to eventually come back to buy. And this type of information giving works well in getting people to give information, such as filling in a form of data.

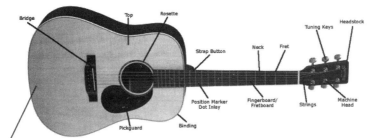

Useful information at a Web site can act
as a gift and thereby trigger reciprocity.

REWARD VERSUS RECIPROCITY

In a another study (Gamberini et.al., 2007), researchers tested reward vs. reciprocity. They used a Web site that provided useful information about different formats for media files, definitions of media files, when to use each format, and so on. In the Reward Condition, visitors could access the information by first completing a form that asked for their names, addresses, and other demographic information. In the Reciprocity Condition, visitors could immediately access the information, and then they were later asked to fill out the form. Visitors in the Reciprocity Condition were twice as likely to fill out the form than those who experienced the Reward Condition.

IT'S OKAY TO ASK FOR THE RECIPROCAL ACTION

NO STRINGS ATTACHED is powerful, but it is also okay to ask for a reciprocal action—especially when you provide useful information.

What To Look For...

Acoustic Guitar

Body Style:
Acoustic guitars come in a variety of sizes and shapes, from small travel size, to jumbo, to dreadnought. The body style in an acoustic guitar determines sound projection and tonal emphasis. Things to consider are tonal quality vs. playing comfort. Some acoustic guitar bodies come in a single cutaway design like the shape of the Gibson Les Paul. This gives access to the higher frets.

Electronics:
Some acoustic guitars come with pickups and preamps built in for playing larger venues where your acoustic sound needs to fill the room. Some instruments have preamps mounted in a hole cut in the side of the instrument, while others mount inside the soundhole. There are systems that combine preamp, microphone, piezo pickups , EQ, and tuners.

Neck:
The concept for necks on acoustic guitars is the same as it is for electrics; the size of your hand is key. Generally the thickness and width of the neck is based on the size of the body of the instrument as well as how many frets the neck has. Usually, acoustic necks are listed as 12-fret or 14-fret. This refers to the number of frets clear of the body, not how many overall.

Intonation:
Intonation determines whether or not the notes play in tune as you move up the neck. If the distance between the frets (usually above the 12th fret) is off, the guitar will be incapable of playing in tune and therefore useless as a recording or performance instrument.

Tonewood:
The choice of wood determines the sound of an acoustic guitar. Different types of wood produce different tones, but most guitar makers believe that the top is the most important for determining tonal quality. Spruce is the standard material for tops with Sitka spruce being the most common. The cost of an acoustic guitar increases dramatically based on the rarity of the tonewoods, such as rosewood, but due to decreasing supplies of certain tonewoods, guitar makers are successfully finding alternative materials to make great sounding instruments.

Tuning Machines:
The type of tuning machine your guitar has is very important. This is what allows you to fine tune and hold pitch. Enclosed machine heads resist rust and airborne corrosives, and therefore don't require as much maintenance or replacement as open tuning machines.

Bridge and Fingerboard:
The materials used for bridge and fingerboard do have an effect on sound, but this is minimal compared to the body of the guitar. Put simply, the effects of bridge and fingerboard materials cannot make or break a guitar's sound.

Finish:
Different types of finish can affect the way the wood vibrates, but there is nothing you can do about this. These decisions are make by the guitar maker and they usually choose wisely.

Shop for Acoustic Guitar » »

www.sweetwater.com

This site suggests the reciprocal action right after the useful information.

Even giving visitors recommendations can be seen as a gift (as long as the recommendations are deemed to be useful information to visitors). If visitors love books on rare antiques and they receive notification that a new book on rare antiques has been published, they're likely to consider that notice useful information (and a gift of sorts).

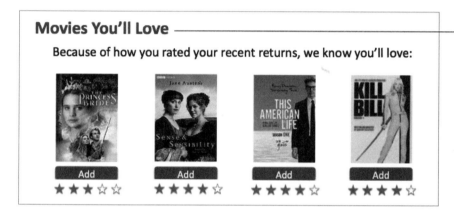

A recommendation can be seen as a gift if the information is helpful.

Showing your visitors other products they might be interested in buying might be seen by them as a gift from you.

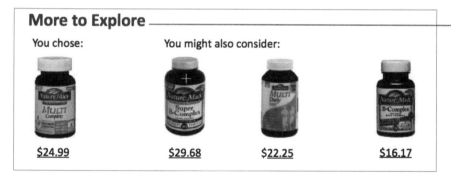

Showing alternative choices can be seen as useful information and a gift.

Here's an idea that is different, but might also trigger reciprocity: A for-profit company can give a donation to a non-profit organization for you, and thereby engender a feeling of indebtedness by you. It's as though they gave a gift "for you," even if they gave it to someone else. Now you feel that you should give something to them since they donated for you.

Sites donating for you are giving you a gift of sorts.

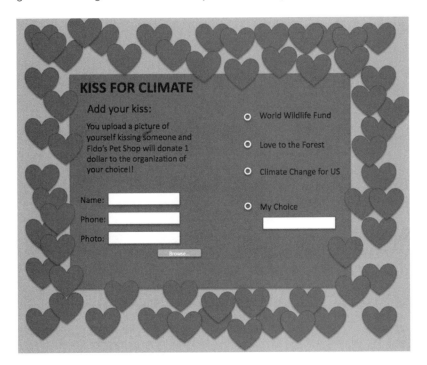

The above image shows an example of this concept. If you take a picture of yourself kissing someone and upload it, the site owners, in turn, will donate to an organization of your choice. This act of goodwill is likely to create a feeling of indebtedness in you because the company has not only acted on your behalf, but they've likely triggered your emotional connection to your favorite organization.

Now you will feel indebted to them (which is what they want). You will want to return the favor or gift, perhaps by being a loyal customer or by visiting their site again.

In some cases, your gift might be your user information — the Name and Phone fields you see in this example. Sites are known to sell or trade this information with other sites that are looking to expand their audience.

Giving a gift triggers indebtedness, which increases the likelihood that others will reciprocate by giving you something.

If you first ask for something that others consider beyond their means and they say no, follow immediately with a more reasonable request, and they are more likely to say yes.

BOTTOM LINE

4

Invoking Scarcity—If Something Seems Unavailable, We Seem to Want It Even More

YOUR COMPANY IS introducing a new product. Everyone gears up. The production line is cranking. The marketing department is letting current and potential customers know that the product will be out the first of the year, and there are plenty to be had. All is good, right?

Wrong. The marketing department should be saying that there are only a limited number available at the first of the year—and they might not be able to fill the demand.

Remember the iPhone introduction? When it came out the first time, there were long lines to get one. Remember when the 3G model came out a year or so later? Same thing: Long lines. Long waits. You can order one, but who knows when you will get it. And Apple implied there might not be enough to go around.

It is the same thing with some brands of hybrid cars. There are long waits. Yet the orders keep coming. If it's scarce, we think it is more valuable and more desirable.

We'll want it more.

> **If there is limited availability of something, we assume it is more valuable, and we want it even more.**

Scarcity works—not just for products, but for information, too. We can read about trends in the computer industry online by searching for articles on Google. Or we can subscribe to a pricey series of reports that cost a lot of money and only a relatively few people get. Which source of information will we think is more accurate? More valuable? Which source will we use when it is time to take action?

> **If we think that information is hard to come by, then we see that information as being more valuable.**

WHICH COOKIES TASTE BEST?

WORCHEL, LEE, AND ADEWOLE (1975) asked people to rate chocolate chip cookies. They put 10 cookies in one jar and two of the same cookies in another jar. The cookies from the two-cookie jar received higher ratings—even though the cookies were exactly the same! Not only that, but if there were a lot of cookies in the jar, and then a short time later most of the cookies were gone, the cookies that were left received an even higher rating than cookies that were in a jar where the number of cookies didn't change

Social validation and scarcity work together (read Chapter 2, "Wanting to Belong: The Power of Social Validation," if you have not already). If we think a lot of other people liked the cookies *and* that there aren't many cookies left, it creates an even stronger pull to action.

ONLY TWO LEFT IN YOUR SIZE!

I DON'T OWN a lot of shoes. I'm not like some people that have entire closets filled with shoes. I have very wide feet, and I like to be comfortable. So shoes are important to me, but I don't own a lot of them. Because my size is hard to find, I am very sensitive to the phrase, "only one left in stock." It's easy to invoke a sense of scarcity in me when it comes to shoes. And the shoes I do buy I end up loving and wearing forever. (In fact, I wear them until they look terrible, but I'm still emotionally attached to them.)

It's easy to invoke scarcity at an e-commerce Web site. If we see the phrase, "only two left in your size" or "only one left in stock," we feel that we'd better hurry up and make the purchase before they are all gone.

Invoking scarcity at a product web site.

Scarcity applies to many types of Web sites. Travel sites make use of it, too. You have to book now to get this fare.

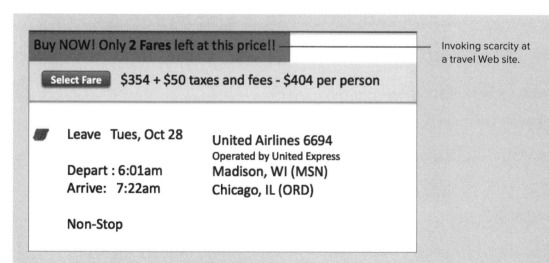

Invoking scarcity at a travel Web site.

OFFER ENDS AT THE
END OF THE MONTH

CAR DEALERSHIPS USE this tactic a lot. A friend of mine told me the story of her recent car purchase. The sales person told her that because it was the last day of the month, the salesperson had to make her quota, so she would knock $5,000 off the price of the car. Not only that, but because there were no "lower" models on the lot, she would give her the "mid-level" model that was sitting on the lot for the same price. But my friend had to buy it right then and there, that very day. The deal would end at the end of the month, which also happened to be the end of that day. My friend drove her new car off the lot later that afternoon. She said she was well aware of the salesperson's tactics, but it didn't matter to my friend. She still fell for it, but she adds, "I love, love, love my new vehicle!"

TODAY ONLY invokes scarcity (of time).

Time can be used to convey scarcity at a Web site. The phrase, "For a limited time only," creates the same scarcity effect.

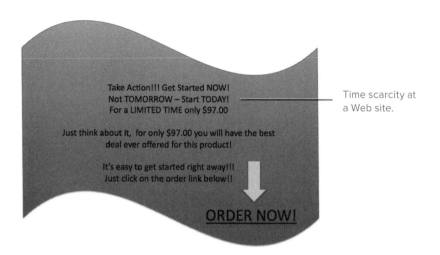

Take Action!!! Get Started NOW!
Not TOMORROW – Start TODAY!
For a LIMITED TIME only $97.00

Just think about it, for only $97.00 you will have the best
deal ever offered for this product!

It's easy to get started right away!!!
Just click on the order link below!!

ORDER NOW!

Time scarcity at
a Web site.

ONLY A SELECT FEW KNOW THIS

DURING BARACK OBAMA'S campaign, you could register at his Web site to become eligible to receive exclusive updates regarding his campaign. For example, you could receive text messages announcing who he had picked to be his Vice Presidential running mate before the general public was made aware of this information.

Being a member invokes special privileges. If only select people will have this information, then the information is valuable.

How many free newsletters do you sign up for at a Web site? If it's free, it's available to just anyone—so it must not be very valuable. But what if there is a price attached? A paid subscription is often just a newsletter you pay money to receive. But it seems more valuable because there's

Be the First to Know

Do you want to know who the Vice-Presidential running mate is going to be? You have helped to build this movement from the bottom up, and you are an essential part of this campaign!

Sign up today and we'll send you an email or text announcing the running mate choice!

Email:
First Name:
Last Name:
Cell Phone:

Submit

a price attached to it. Or perhaps it's available only if you are a "member." If you have to pay or join, the information is that much more difficult to access, and that means it might well be more desirable as a result.

NUTRITION NEWSLETTER

Save over 50%

"The most informative newsletter you'll ever read on the topic of making great choices and avoiding common mistakes"
~Melanie LaBarre– Health and Self Magazine

Yes! I would like to subscribe!!!

◎ 1 Year = $29.95

◎ 2 Years = $39.95

If we pay for the information, then we value it. Valuing it builds customer loyalty.

IF IT COSTS A LOT, IT MUST BE GOOD

A CONCEPT SIMILAR to scarcity is the idea that things that are more expensive (and therefore harder to get—scarce) are of higher quality. We unconsciously tend to want what is expensive. We unconsciously equate expensive to "better."

If it costs more it must be better!

Our Price: $349.99

Our Price: $99.97

SORRY, YOU CAN'T HAVE IT

AND ONE LAST tactic involving scarcity: Ban something altogether. If something is totally inaccessible, then it is really scarce. If something is forbidden or banned, then we *really* want it.

Iraq for Sale Banned Excerpts

On May 10th, 2007, this video was banned in Congress.

0:02/1:51

If it's banned, then it is really desirable.

If something is scarce, it will seem more desirable and more valuable to us.

Showing a limited quantity in stock, or a limited time frame that something is available, invokes scarcity. Scarcity motivates us to act.

Not only products can be scarce. Access to information might be hard to get, and therefore will make that information seem more valuable to us as well.

BOTTOM LINE

5

Choosing Carefully—Given Too Many Choices, We Freeze (and Then We Don't Choose at All)

AS I STARTED writing this book, I decided I should buy an external hard drive to backup these chapters. I went to the NewEgg.com Web site to make a purchase. It took me at least 10 visits and over three hours to make this purchase. Why? Because every time I went to visit the site, there were dozens—no, make that hundreds—of hard drives to choose from. And they were pretty much all the same. All the same size, all the same capacity, all the same price. They differed in shape and color. That purchase took me a long time.

One interesting thing about choices is that we think we want a lot of them, but in actuality, a lot of choices hinders our decision-making process. If given a choice between a few alternatives or numerous choices, we will most likely want as many choices as possible. But research shows it doesn't help us as much as we think. This is a classic case where what we think we want (conscious brain) is just plain wrong. We really don't make better decisions with more choices, but we think we do. Too many choices just makes us freeze and then we make no choice at all.

> *We say we want a lot of choices, but the reality is that when we have a lot of choices, we can't decide.*

IN A JAM

IYENGAR AND LEPPER (2000) tested the theory that if we're provided with too many choices, we don't choose at all. Experimenters set up booths at a busy upscale grocery store in Menlo Park, California, and posed as store employees. They alternated the product selections on the table. Half of the time, there were six choices of fruit jam for shoppers to taste. Half of the time, there were 24 jars of jam to taste.

Did it make a difference how many jars there were? Yes, it did. When there were 24 jars of jam on the table, 60 percent of shoppers passing the table stopped and tasted jam. When there were six jars of jam on the table, only 40 percent stopped to taste. So does that mean that more choices are a good thing?

But wait, there's more.

You would think that people would taste more varieties of jam when the table had 24 flavors. But they didn't. People tasted one to two varieties, whether there were six or 24 choices available.

And how did varying the selection influence purchases? Of the shoppers who stopped at the table with six jars, 30 percent actually purchased the brand of jam they had tried. Of those who stopped at the table with 24 jars, only three percent purchased jam.

So what do we learn from this? A bigger selection attracted a bigger crowd, but that crowd purchased fewer products than the group presented with fewer choices.

To give you an example of the numbers, if 100 shoppers came by (they actually had more than that in the study, but 100 makes the calculations easy for our purposes):

- At the table with 24 jars, 60 stopped to taste jam but only two purchased jam.
- At the table with six jars, 40 tasted jam and 12 purchased jam.

Less is more.

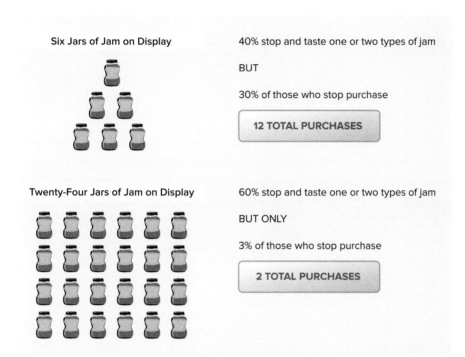

Six Jars of Jam on Display

40% stop and taste one or two types of jam

BUT

30% of those who stop purchase

12 TOTAL PURCHASES

Twenty-Four Jars of Jam on Display

60% stop and taste one or two types of jam

BUT ONLY

3% of those who stop purchase

2 TOTAL PURCHASES

More jars means more people stop by, but fewer people purchase.

Lots of choices will grab our attention, but too many choices overwhelm us—to the point where we likely won't buy at all.

THIS PANTYHOSE IS SOFTER

A REALTOR FRIEND of mine says prospective home buyers come to her with a list of what's important to them in buying a house, yet she doesn't fully believe their list truly reflects what's important to them. Her experience is that individuals fall in love with a house even though the house fails to meet many of the criteria they have on their "must have" list.

Why?

We like to think that our choices are based on a logical weighing of one choice versus another, but there is a lot of research that shows that our choices are not logical. In fact, we aren't consciously aware of why we are choosing one item over another. And after we make a choice, we can't even accurately explain why we made the choice we did. We will try to make up a reason, but it probably isn't accurate.

Wilson (2002) showed people four types of pantyhose and asked them to select the type they would prefer to buy. People had definite preferences. (Most of them chose the pair that was farthest to the right on the table.) What they didn't know was that all the pantyhose were exactly alike.

When asked why they chose the one on the far right, they provided a variety of reasons, including "it's softer" or "it's stronger."

HOW TO RUIN YOUR RELATIONSHIP

IN FACT, THERE is some research that shows that a logical analysis of a purchase, or an analysis of your likes and dislikes, may be a harmful thing to engage in.

Wilson and Kraft (1993) asked couples to analyze their relationships and write lists of why they liked the person they were involved with. Wilson then compared the longevity of the relationship in these couples to the longevity of relationships in a control group that was not asked to logically analyze their relationship. Analyzing the relationships resulted in the relationship ending sooner than the relationships where couples were *not* asked for an analysis.

Analyzing doesn't just ruin relationships, but it also seems to ruin your satisfaction with the purchases you make. Wilson (1993) studied individuals buying art posters:

- Group A analyzed why they liked and didn't like five art posters.

- Group B did not do any analysis.

Each individual in each group then picked one poster to take home. Two weeks later, researchers contacted them to see how happy they were with their choices. Those in Group B, who didn't analyze the art they took home, were happier with their choices than those in Group A (who had analyzed their art).

Dijksterhuis and van Olden (2005) performed the study again, but they added a few twists. Participants were told the study focused on evaluating art. Everyone in the study was brought in to look at art posters, one at a time, for 15 seconds on a computer screen. Then, after looking at the posters, they were assigned to one of three conditions where they performed more tasks:

- In the **Conscious Thought condition**, participants looked at each poster one by one on the computer screen and were asked to analyze carefully whether they liked each poster and why or why not. They were given paper and pen to record their analyses. Then all the posters appeared on one screen, and they were asked to pick the one they liked the best.

- In the **Unconscious Thought condition**, participants engaged in a different task—they worked on anagrams—for the same amount of time. Then they were shown the posters again, all placed on a single screen, and asked which one they liked the best.

- In the **Immediate Decision condition**, participants were shown a single screen showing all the art posters and asked which poster they liked the most.

At the end of the experiment, the participants could choose a poster to take home. The researchers hypothesized that the Unconscious Thought participants (who worked on anagrams) had made their decisions unconsciously and would be most satisfied with their choices.

They were correct!

It seems that if we make our choice unconsciously, without conscious processing, then we stick with it over time. If we spend more time and logically analyze why we're choosing what we're choosing, we're less satisfied over time with our choices.

WATCHING THE BRAIN LIGHT UP

YOU HAVE BEEN saving for a new car. You've got enough money saved to purchase a new Honda Civic. It's a reliable car. It gets great mileage. You think it's cute. If you save longer, you'll be able to get the flashier Honda sports car (the S2000)—but it costs twice as much. You'd really like the S2000.

Which car will you purchase? Well, it might depend on where you are and what you are doing when you are trying to decide.

A relatively new technology called **functional Magnetic Resonance Imaging** (**fMRI**) lets us see into the brain while it is working. When certain parts of the brain are active, those parts will show up as colored lights on a computer display. A group of researchers (McClure et al, 2004) asked individuals to choose between certain money rewards. They could get a small amount of money ($5) now or a larger amount of money ($40) later. Researchers varied the amount of money, how difficult it was to calculate when you would get what amount, and how long participants would have to wait to get the larger amount (one week vs. two weeks).

When participants thought about waiting, and when they calculated how much they would get if they waited, the pre-frontal cortex (new brain) lit up. But when they thought about getting the money right away, the mid brain lit up—especially the area of the mid brain that involves pleasure. Apparently, our unconscious, emotional brain (mid brain) is activated when we imagine getting something that we think would be nice, pleasant, and rewarding—especially if we get it right away.

This implies that if we are making a decision about buying something, we will be swayed by whether we can have it right away. The mid brain will compete with the new brain about whether to wait.

If we are making a decision with the product right there in front of us, then we will be swayed by the product itself—the look, smell, or feel of it. Buying something on the Internet may not have that same immediacy and allure to the mid brain. In order for the mid brain to get engaged and say "now, now, now," and in order for us to take action right away, something at the site has to get the attention of our mid brain.

GET IT RIGHT AWAY

IF WE SEE that we'll get what we want right away, that will speak to the mid brain and encourage us to act.

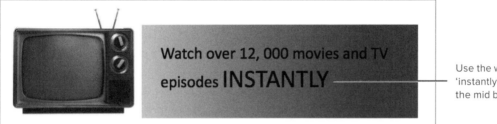

Use the word 'instantly' to capture the mid brain.

For the mid brain, it's all about immediacy. If the Web site can't promise it immediately, the next best thing is to let us know it will be there very soon. Notice that in the message that follows, there is immediacy about when it will be delivered (tomorrow) and when you should order it (in the next 19 minutes).

Want it delivered tomorrow??
Order it in the next **19 minutes** and choose Overnight-Shipping at checkout. <u>See Details.</u>

The mid brain pays attention when it sees that it can get it by a certain date, and when there are only a few minutes left.

With sites like Apple's iTunes, we can order and download music instantly. This is irresistible and has revolutionized how we buy music. Instead of driving to a store to purchase an entire CD, we can buy only the songs we want—instantly and with only a few clicks of a mouse.

Song	Time	Band	Album	Price	
West Bank	3:22	Story of the Sea	Lunar	.99	Buy Song
The Beast	4:33	Story of the Sea	For Callum	.99	Buy Song
Distillery	3:54	Story of the Sea	For Callum	.99	Buy Song

Buying music instantly speaks to the mid brain.

TALK TO THE OLD BRAIN

IMAGINE THIS SCENARIO: You've just bought a digital camera for $689.99. Now you realize that you didn't buy a carrying case. You don't want to walk around with it in your pocket or bag, since it could get scratched. So you go online to shop for a camera case. Are you going to buy the nice, all-weather camera backpack for $89.95? Or are you going to save some money by purchasing a cloth case for only $9.97? The amount of $89.95 for a camera case seems a bit much. That's because you are comparing it with a cloth camera case for $9.97.

When presented alongside much less expensive cases, the $89.95 case seems a little steep. In this case, you'll probably choose a less expensive model.

All weather camera backpack
Buy New: $89.95

Camera Case with Strap
Buy New: $19.95

Mini-Cloth Camera Case
Buy New: $9.97

If you had purchased the camera case when you first bought the camera, you probably would have chosen a nicer and more expensive case. In that situation, you are comparing $89.95 to the price of the $689.99 camera. Then $90 seems like a bargain compared to $689.99. And how does a $29.99 price grab you? In the example that follows, you'd likely purchase the seemingly cheap case for $29.99. And then you'll put a logical reason on top of the decision, since you have to protect your expensive $689.99 investment.

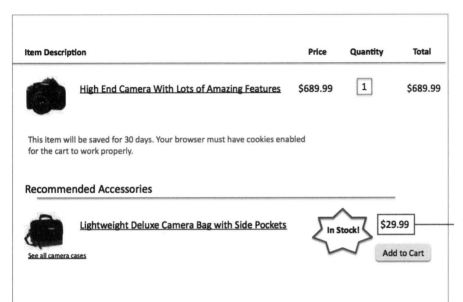

Item Description	Price	Quantity	Total
High End Camera With Lots of Amazing Features	$689.99	1	$689.99

This item will be saved for 30 days. Your browser must have cookies enabled for the cart to work properly.

Recommended Accessories

Lightweight Deluxe Camera Bag with Side Pockets	In Stock!	$29.99
See all camera cases		Add to Cart

When we've invested nearly $700 in a camera, the $29.99 price tag for a camera case seems 'cheap' to us.

This is an example of **up-sell**. In order for us to be influenced by this up-sell, the extra accessories have to appear at the time we are making the larger purchase.

The old brain is engaged if there is choice decision that involves contrast. The old brain is looking for basics. Big versus small; expensive versus inexpensive. It will make instant decisions about good and bad based on contrast.

FIRST IS BEST: THE ORDER EFFECT

YOU GO TO a Web site to buy a tent for camping. You answer some questions about the type of camping you plan to do. The site then recommends four tents that best match your use and compares the four tents based on 10 attributes (how waterproof they are, how much they weigh, how much air ventilation they have, and so on). Two of the four tents are "best buys" for the attributes that are important to you. Which tent will you buy?

Felfernig (2007) set up a research study to find out. Even though there were 10 attributes that the tents were compared on, participants focused only on two or three attributes. The researchers varied the order in which the tents appeared on the page: first, second, third, or fourth. It turns out that the most important attribute was not whether the tent was waterproof or if it had plenty of air ventilation. The most important attribute was the order in which the tents appeared on the page! Participants disregarded attributes and simply picked whichever tent was the first one to show on-screen. In fact, they picked the first tent 2.5 times more than any other. They chose the first tent 200 times; they chose the other three tents (combined) only 60 times. This is called an **order effect**.

The participants explained their choices, however, based on the logical decisions they thought they were making. For example, they explained the choice of tent #1 by saying, "This tent is the most waterproof." They thought they were weighing *all* the attributes of *all* the tents, but in reality they were considering only a few attributes—and even those attributes didn't matter. All that mattered was an unconscious reaction to which tent showed up first.

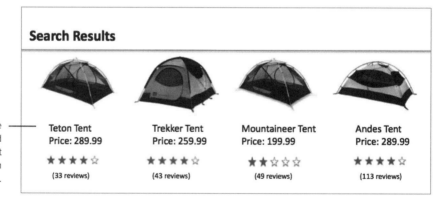

Search Results

Teton Tent	Trekker Tent	Mountaineer Tent	Andes Tent
Price: 289.99	Price: 259.99	Price: 199.99	Price: 289.99
★★★★☆	★★★★☆	★★☆☆☆	★★★★☆
(33 reviews)	(43 reviews)	(49 reviews)	(113 reviews)

We tend to ignore our preferences and simply pick the first item that appears on the page.

If you have a Web site, look carefully at the algorithms of what products appear in which order. Make sure the first item is the one you'd like to sell the most.

We think we want a lot of choices, but lots of choices just makes us unable to take any action at all.

We can focus only on one or two product attributes at a time.

BOTTOM LINE

If we think we can get something right away, that notion will be a strong pull to take action and buy right away.

If you want someone to choose a particular product at a Web site, list that product first.

6

It's All About *You:* Speaking to the
Self-Centered, Unconscious Mind

Photo Credit: Katie Ricard

YOU ARE WALKING down a dark street. You are all alone. You hear footsteps behind you. Your heart starts beating faster. You can hear the blood throbbing in your veins.

Do I have your attention now?

You, you, you, you, you, you, you.

You are hungry. *You* are cold. *You* are bored. *Your* ideas are important. *You* want this. *You* want that.

You, you, you, you, you, you, you.

Your primitive old brain is wired to care about *you.* To the old brain, everything is all about *you. You* are all that matters. In the scenario where you're walking down the dark street, I grabbed your attention in multiple ways:

● First, it was a story (for more information about stories, see Chapter 10).

● Second, it sounded dangerous, which your old brain is very interested in.

● Third, it started with the word "you" and included seven references to "you" or "your" within only five sentences.

Your old brain is wired to keep you alive. It's all about survival. Therefore, nothing is more important to your old brain than you. Your old brain is constantly scanning the surroundings looking for anything that might be a threat to your survival, as well as looking for opportunities to eat and to have sex.

I apologize about being blunt, but this is the reality of the old brain. Physical survival, food, and sex are really what the old brain focuses on. It is therefore very skilled at noticing what has changed. It is scanning all the time looking for changes and then quickly evaluating any changes in your environment in terms of survival, food, or sex.

The old brain is constantly scanning the environment looking for any changes that signal danger, food, or sex.

DANGER, SEX, AND FOOD

READ THIS paragraph:

"This software has many built-in features that allow for photos to be uploaded, organized, and stored. Photos can be searched for with only a few steps."

Now read this paragraph:

"You can upload your photos quickly, organize them any way you want to, and then store them so that they are easy to share with your friends. You can find any photo with only a few steps."

Which product would you buy? You'd likely buy the one that says "you" and "your." This is not a conscious decision. Your non-conscious old brain will tell you that the second product is better for *you*.

In many cultures, being so self-focused is seen as negative. It is classified as selfishness. And certainly there are times when you want to be unselfish. But it is a fact of nature that if you want to get and hold the attention of humans, and if you want to get them to take action, you need to engage the old brain.

Basically, you have only a few ways to engage the old brain: danger, sex, and food.

Do something threatening

Since a major job of the old brain is to keep us from harm, anything threatening our survival will get the old brain's attention. The threat doesn't have to be directed at us. Even watching a movie or an ad (not a real situation) of someone *else* in harm (not you) will set off all the alarm bells of the old brain. So if we are watching a video of a scary car chase scene, our old brain is yelling, "Be careful, be careful!"

When the old brain sounds an alarm, all of our information processing and emotional processing systems are on high alert and highly functioning. This means that anything happening while we're on high alert will be processed deeply and emotionally in our memory (Medina, 2008). There is an entire branch of marketing now focusing on activating the old brain and then feeding it product information.

As such, there are television commercials that use a dangerous situation (for example, a car chase) that culminates with someone receiving a particular brand of soda or a particular credit card. The idea is that all of our systems are on heightened alert, so we will remember the product, and we will also attach strong emotions to it. In terms of attention-getting and deep-encoding in memory, it actually doesn't matter if we are scared or exhilarated; it doesn't matter if the emotions we are feeling are "positive" or "negative." What matters is that our systems are all on high alert.

> **We pay attention to anything that happens when we are in an emotionally arousing situation. We also remember it more deeply.**

Because the old brain cares about safety and danger, any pictures or headlines that look or sound frightening will automatically get our attention.

Show food

We pay attention to food. In order to grab our attention with food, the food should be shown prominently. Showing a picture of people sitting at a restaurant implies food, but to capture the old brain's attention, the food must be very obvious.

If a Web site is about food, it will easily grab and hold our attention. What's important is that it shows luscious photos of the food.

Food Web sites will grab our attention easily as long as there are gorgeous pictures of the food.

Even a site that is not necessarily selling food might be able to use the allure of food to grab and hold our attention.

Pictures of food are effective even at Web sites that aren't selling food.

Imply sex

We all know that sex, or the implication of sex, is a powerful attention-getting technique. Sex is so powerful as an attention-getting technique that it can snag our attention with even the subtlest of associations. A certain look to the eyes, a flash of skin—these are all powerful enough to engage our attention.

Even just a subtle look in the eyes can imply sex and draw our attention.

Photo Credit: Katie Ricard

DON'T LET THEM GET BORED

IF A WEB site is about sex or food or danger, it will probably engage the old brain and grab attention. But what about sites that have nothing to do with sex, food, or danger? Can they grab attention, too?

Is there anything else that will grab the attention of the old brain?

All you need is change

Because our old brain is constantly scanning the environment, any change in the environment will be noticed. This is why banner ads that move or change at a Web site are so effective at getting attention (and also why they are so annoying, because they keep changing—and every time they change, we just *have* to look at them). But banner ads are not a good way to provide change at a Web site. Banner ads are good for the product or company being advertised in the banner ad because they attract attention, but they're not necessarily good for the Web site owner because they draw attention away from the rest of the page.

Banner ads are not the only thing that can change on a Web site. Many Web sites have other information that changes or moves (for example, scrolling products or a video that starts up automatically).

These banner ads and movie trailers move and scroll and start automatically. They will both be effective in drawing attention to them, although we may find them annoying.

Any change on the site will grab the attention of the old brain. You can use photos that cycle through or even headlines that change. For example, Borders often uses a scrolling banner of popular books on their home page. WebMD uses photos and headlines that change every five seconds, highlighting articles that you can click on for more information. And ESPN has multiple locations on their Web site that change: a banner at the top is animated, a video plays automatically on the right, and towards the bottom there is a changing display of sports headlines with photos.

The upside is that if something changes at the site every few seconds, our old brain—and hence our attention—will be engaged. The downside is that because our attention is constantly drawn to that part of the page, we have a hard time looking at (or focusing on) anything else. Also, there is data that suggests young people tolerate this kind of movement well, but older people find it so distracting and annoying that they might leave. Web sites should be aware of their audiences and use movement judiciously.

All you need is *you*

As powerful as movement is at grabbing and holding attention at a Web site, it's not all that you can do. Just by simply using the word *you*, you will get the attention of the old brain.

Using the word "you" is an automatic way to grab the attention of the old brain. Here we've circled all the times that the word "you" appears on the page.

Are YOU ready for a new YOU?

Activity is an important part of a healthy lifestyle. When you're ready, you can find the activity that is right for YOU.

Stop doing everything for everyone else and take time to do something for YOU!

After all, it's the only body you get.

The old brain cares about *you*. It cares about protecting you, feeding you, and helping you to reproduce.

If you want to grab someone's attention, you need to get the attention of the old brain by having something change, by showing food, by implying sex, or by using the word *you*.

BOTTOM LINE

7

Building Commitment—We Want to Think We're Consistent

SOMEONE KNOCKS on your door. You recognize him as a kid from your neighborhood. He is selling popcorn as a fund-raiser for a club he is a member of at school. The club is trying to go to the state convention. How do you react? It depends on the story, or persona, you have of yourself when it comes to topics such as school, fund-raising, and your relationship to your neighborhood. Here's one story you might relate to:

> *"I'm a very busy person. When I'm at home I want to relax, not get bombarded with people at the door selling things. I don't like it when people bother me at home with these fund-raising schemes. The schools should pay for these trips and not make us buy this overpriced popcorn. This poor kid isn't to blame, but I'm not going to buy the popcorn because it just perpetuates this behavior. Someone has got to act right on this. I'm the kind of person who does what is right on principle. I'm going to say no nicely, but firmly."*

Or maybe you can relate to this story:

> *"Oh, isn't that great that the kids are going to the state convention. I remember when I went on a similar trip when I was in high school. It was really fun. Maybe not all that educational, but definitely fun! I'm the kind of person who encourages students to have lots of experiences outside of our own neighborhood. I am the kind of person who supports the school. I'll buy some popcorn and help this kid out."*

Or maybe you can relate to this story:

> *"It kind of annoys me that there are always these kids selling things. But this is part of being a good neighbor. I'm part of the community. I am a good citizen of our neighborhood. I'll buy the popcorn because that's what a good community member would do."*

We have an idea formed in our minds about who we are, and what's important to us. Essentially we have a "story" operating about ourselves at all times. Stories are powerful, as you'll learn in Chapter 10.

We tell ourselves stories about ourselves. We have "self-personas."

We tell ourselves stories about ourselves, and then we tell those same stories to others. We will take action based on one of the stories, or personas, we have about ourselves. We actually have more than one persona. We have different personas for different aspects of ourselves in relation to others. For example, there is a persona we have as a husband or wife, another persona we have as a parent, another persona at work, and yet another persona that defines our relationship with the neighborhood we live in. We make decisions based on staying true to our personas. Most of this decision-making based on personas happens unconsciously. Some aspects of personas are conscious or might even be pulled into consciousness, but most of the time the personas are under the surface.

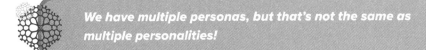

We have multiple personas, but that's not the same as multiple personalities!

These self-personas are important in decision-making because we strive to be consistent in our decision-making. These personas don't have to be exactly alike, but we do strive for some consistency among these personas. There is a drive to make the personas "stick." We will make decisions in order to have our personas stay consistent. This means that there is a higher likelihood that someone will take a particular action if a persona is "activated."

> *It is more likely that someone will take a particular action if one of their personas is activated.*

Once we make one decision consistent with one of the personas, we will try to stay consistent with that persona. We will be more likely to make a decision or take an action if it is consistent with that story or persona.

ONE SMALL STEP...

DO WE EVER make a decision or take an action that isn't totally consistent with an existing persona or story we have? If the action is small (just a little different from the existing persona), it might be possible to convince us to take the action. Once we take *that* action, we actually will adjust our persona a little to fit. That means the next thing we are asked to do along those same lines will fit the new persona, and it will be easier to get us to take action.

> *If you ask someone to commit to something small first, then it will be easier to get a larger commitment from them later.*

WANT TO COVER YOUR LAWN WITH A BIG UGLY SIGN?

WHAT IF SOMEONE knocked on your door and asked you if you would be willing to put a huge, and not very well constructed, billboard on your front lawn that said in large block lettering: DRIVE CAREFULLY. Do you think you would agree? Well, most people in Palo Alto, California, who were asked to do so in a research study in 1966 said no.

Freedman and Fraser (1966) had a researcher pose as a volunteer and go door-to-door asking homeowners to allow just such a sign to be installed in their front yards. They were shown a photo of the sign that would be installed. The signs were quite large (they essentially would take over the front yard) and were fairly ugly. This was not an attractive object to have in their yards! Fewer than 20 percent agreed to have the signs installed in their yards. No surprise there. (Well, actually it is surprising that as many as 20 percent would agree at all.) That was the control group (Group A) of the experiment.

Here's how the rest of the experiment went:

- In Group B, people were first contacted by an experimenter who asked them to put a small (three-inch) sign in the back windows of their cars that read Drive Carefully. Then, three weeks later, a different experimenter showed up to inquire about their interest in having a large DRIVE CAREFULLY sign installed in their yards.

- In Group C, people were first contacted by an experimenter who asked them to sign a petition to "Keep California Beautiful." Then three weeks later, a different experimenter showed up to inquire about their interest in having a large DRIVE CAREFULLY sign installed in their yards.

In the control group (Group A) only 20 percent agreed to have the large DRIVE CAREFULLY signs installed in their yards. What about Groups B and C?

In Group B, which had been asked to first put the small Drive Carefully signs in their car windows and then were approached later to put the large signs in their yards, 76 percent said yes to signs in their yards. For Group C, which had been asked first to sign a petition to Keep California Beautiful (a totally different cause than Drive Carefully), 46 percent agreed to the big ugly signs. It's important to note that in both B and C, different experimenters returned to make the second request—people in those groups were not agreeing simply because they had a relationship of any sort with the person asking.

So 20 percent vs. 46 percent... 20 percent vs. 76 percent.... Why were people much more willing to put a big ugly sign in their yards in these two other conditions?

By agreeing to the request to put the small Drive Carefully sign in the back windows of their cars, a persona was activated in Group B. They were telling themselves the story that they were people who cared about the community at large; they cared about safety. So when they were later asked about installing the big ugly signs, well, for most people that particular request now fit the persona they had about themselves.

With Group C, where people were first asked to sign a petition to "Keep California Beautiful," the petition activated a persona that said "I'm a person who cares about the community," but it didn't necessarily activate a persona that said "I'm a person who cares about safety." When they were asked later to do something a little bit different (to install the huge DRIVE CAREFULLY sign in their yards), that request was only somewhat consistent with the original persona that was activated. The "I'm a person who cares about the community" persona was shared with both requests, but the "I'm a person who cares about safety" was missing. The agreement was double that of Group A (46 percent, compared to 20 percent), but still not as high as the condition of Group B (76 percent).

If you want someone to take action, you need to get a commitment first to something small that will activate a persona, and then you need to ask for a commitment to something larger later. And the more public you can get that commitment (like putting a sign in your car window), the stronger the persona change will be. Making a commitment silently to yourself (for example, telling yourself that you care about the community, but not showing this idea to others) is not as strong as saying the commitment aloud to someone else or taking an action like signing a petition (or posting a sign).

SIGN ON THE DOTTED LINE

IF WE MAKE a commitment publicly, or write it down, the commitment and consistency effect is even stronger.

Deutsch and Gerard (1955) asked people to estimate the length of some lines. They were looking at the effect that others might have on decision-making. They had other people who were part of the experiment estimate the length of the line incorrectly. Would the subjects go along with the incorrect estimates they were hearing from others, or would they stick (commit) to the answer they felt was correct? If you read Chapter 2 on social validation, you won't be surprised to discover that estimates were influenced by the lengths people heard from others.

I think this study is interesting, though, in light of some other findings. In addition to looking at group influence, Deutsch and Gerard also looked at whether there were situations in which *commitment* to a decision would be stronger.

- Before hearing what others had to say on the length of the line, Group 1 wrote their estimates on paper. They were told *not* to sign the paper, and that they would not be turning in the sheets of paper.

- Group 2 wrote their estimates on a "magic pad," and then lifted a sheet and the estimate was erased without anyone seeing it.

- Group 3 was told to write their estimates on paper, to sign their papers, and they were told that their papers would be collected at the end of the experiment.

Would the groups vary in terms of how strongly they stuck to their commitment of the length of the line?

Group 2 was most likely to change their decisions and to give incorrect estimates. Groups 1 and 3 reacted the same way. They were five times less likely to change their answers. They were more committed to their original estimates, regardless of what they heard others say.

Signing their names or being told they were going to hand in their estimates did not seem to make a difference. Just the act of writing it on a piece of paper was enough to make them commit.

Writing something down is a powerful act of commitment.

FIRST AN IPOD, THEN A MAC?

FOR AS LONG as there were PCs, I was a PC type person. My husband was a Mac person. We would archly defend the technology of choice. Over time, I learned to just ignore his Mac comments, and he learned to use a PC, since that was what we had at home (his Mac was at his office, where he is a news-paper editor).

Then the iPod came out, and I decided that would be a great gizmo to have while exercising. I actually did feel a twinge of dissonance when I broke a little bit from my non-Apple, all-PC persona to buy an Apple product. But it was only a type of MP3 player really, right? So it was a small action away from my usual persona. Not too drastic.

But it was a crack in my PC persona. I was now a PC person who used an Apple product. I loved my iPod. And over time, my PC persona began to give way. I was becoming a person who believed in Apple products. This created a huge amount of dissonance, and when it came time to purchase a new laptop, I dissipated the dissonance by buying a Mac laptop. I had effortlessly erased years of a PC persona, because my persona had already been sliding that way, even though I was not conscious of the slide until it came time for the larger purchase.

Whether Apple did this on purpose or not, the introduction of the iPod was a masterful lead-in to getting people to switch from PCs to Macs.

WHEN COMMITMENTS ARE STRONGEST

CIALDINI (2007) REPORTS that if a public commitment is not "owned" by a person, and is mainly made to gain a large reward, the individual is not deeply committed and will not show deep commitment in future behavior. If we believe that we have voluntarily chosen to act in a certain way because of our inner beliefs instead of strong outside pressures, we feel more committed. A large reward, for example, may lead us to action, but it will not create inner responsibility for the action, and we won't feel committed to the action.

Growing commitment

Interestingly, you can "grow" commitment. Cialdini (2007) reports that a mild admonition or small threat of punishment can encourage us to behave in certain ways. After we do behave that way, we have a tendency to want to be consistent, and may therefore take personal responsibility for the behavior, which then leads to deep change. The pressure for consistency causes the commitment to deepen.

When you go through pain

I went from an iPod to a Mac to an iPhone. The transition from PC to Mac was not easy (too many years on PCs, I guess), but I was determined to stick with it until I was comfortable. In fact, the harder it was, the more determined I got. My first iPhone had problems. I had to send it back. I had waited almost a year to get an iPhone. The replacement worked better, but it still didn't work correctly. I've called AppleCare once already, and we solved the problem—for about an hour. Then things got worse, and I couldn't even make phone calls. However, I was very forgiving. I still liked my iPhone, even though I couldn't get it to work right. I was sure it would all get taken care of and would all work out. I would never have been that patient with any other cell phone. But I'm committed to Apple now. It took me years to make the switch to Apple, and getting the iPhone was a long and arduous process. You would think that these problems would erode my commitment to Apple, but it did just the opposite. It strengthened my commitment. (By the way, the phone is working better, but I still have some issues. Really, I'm sure I'll solve them soon.)

FROM A BUCKET OF WATER TO A CASH DONATION?

IN ORDER TO get us to take a particular action on a Web site, the Web site will have to activate a persona that would take that action.

Let's say you are not someone who normally gives money to charities that provide aid to other countries, but that you *are* a person who enjoys playing trivia quizzes. A friend forwards you a link to a Web site where you play a trivia quiz, and every correct answer results in a bucket of clean water being donated to a country in need of clean water. You decide to try it to see how your trivia skills stack up. At the end of the session, you are told you just donated 50 buckets of clean water to another country. Now you are a person who donates aid. If you are then asked to pass the Web site on to another person, or to donate money for more aid, you are more likely to take either of these actions, since your persona has been expanded.

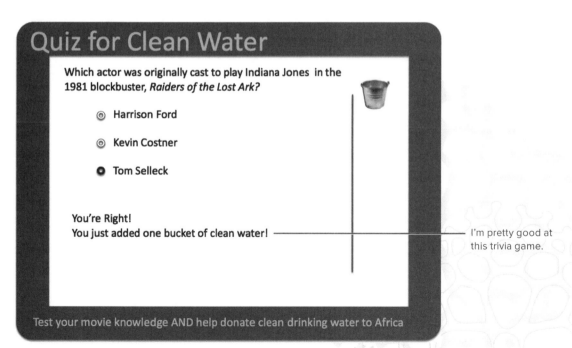

Quiz for Clean Water

This classic thriller, first shown in the summer of 1975, made people very afraid of:

- ◎ The shower
- ● The ocean
- ◎ Demons

You're Right!
You now have 50 buckets of water !

Test your movie knowledge AND help donate clean drinking water to Africa

Hmmm, I've just donated some water.

Quiz for Clean Water

This classic thriller, first shown in the summer of 1975, made people very afraid of:

- ◎ The shower
- ● The ocean
- ◎ Demons

You're Right!
You now have 50 buckets of water !

Help us give the children of Africa clean water to drink. Donate now!

Test your movie knowledge AND help donate clean drinking water to Africa

Now the site can ask you for a request that is in line with someone who donates.

WHEN IS A SURVEY MORE THAN A SURVEY?

YOU GO TO an e-commerce Web site and buy a shirt. After the purchase, you are asked to fill out a survey. If you liked the site, you will respond positively to the survey questions. The owners of the Web site might really be trying to get your opinion so they can improve the site. But whether they realize it or not, they also just got you to commit to the site. Although you probably weren't announcing your reaction to the site to the whole world, you did provide a response (more than just in your head). Any time we state positive feelings or opinions about a product or service to someone else, even if that *someone else* is a faceless person behind a Web site, we have committed. And that commitment increases the likelihood that we will engage with that Web site again.

> *Surveys can be used not only to gather data from customers, but also to elicit a public statement of support that will help clinch commitment.*

WHEN A REVIEW IS MORE THAN A REVIEW

THE MORE PUBLIC the commitment, the more it will stick—and the more it will affect current and future behavior. Completing an anonymous survey is better than no commitment at all, but it is still fairly hidden. To strengthen the level of commitment, Web site owners can heighten the public element of the action. A review posted at the Web site for others to read is a stronger public statement of commitment. If you have written a review of a product or a testimonial of the company, you have made a more public commitment. You are saying, "I am a person who believes in this product," or, "I am a person who donates to this organization," or "I am a person who buys from this company." (This assumes that the review is positive, of course. Writing a negative review is just as strong of a commitment, but in the opposite direction.)

Writing a review is an act of public commitment.

www.discountdance.com

Reviews act on others as a form of social validation (see Chapter 2), but they also act on the self as a form of commitment. If we write a positive review, we will then want to stay consistent, and that means we will take more action to interact with the site, the company, and the organization. If you want to build commitment to your brand, your company, or a product, then make sure you give visitors the opportunity to write a review.

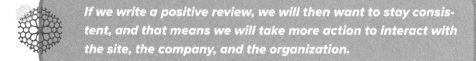

If we write a positive review, we will then want to stay consistent, and that means we will take more action to interact with the site, the company, and the organization.

Ask people to commit to an idea verbally or, even better, in writing.

If possible, do this in stages, so that you are asking for the commitment first and then, at a later date, asking for an action that is consistent with that commitment.

BOTTOM LINE

Getting people to write or sign something strengthens commitment.

If we go through a difficult experience, we will be even more committed to the product or affiliation.

8

Using Similarity, Attractiveness, and Association: Are We the Same?

YOU ARE in a store looking at a refrigerator that you are thinking about buying. A sales person walks up to you and starts discussing the merits of the model you are looking at. Which of the following is true?

a) You are more likely to listen to the salesperson and make the purchase if the sales person is similar to you in characteristics such as age and dress.

b) You are more likely to listen to the salesperson and make the purchase if you find the sales person to be attractive.

c) You are more likely to listen to the salesperson and make the purchase if the sales person is different than you.

d) Age and appearance do not affect your sales decision.

e) Both b and c.

f) Both a and b.

The correct answer is f. You are more likely to listen to the sales person and make the purchase if the sales person is similar to you in characteristics such as age and dress and if you find the sales person to be attractive.

You are more likely to listen to and buy from someone who is like you and someone you find attractive.

You might be thinking, "Well, other people might be affected by such super-ficial considerations, but not me." But we are all affected by what someone looks like. And our decisions about who to talk with, whether to believe or listen to them, and whether to buy products from them are definitely affected by the cues that tell us whether the person is "like" us and whether the person is "attractive" to us.

FLEE, EAT, OR HAVE SEX?

WE MAKE THESE decisions very quickly, and the decisions are not immediate-ly conscious. In the book *Strangers to Ourselves: The Adaptive Unconscious* (2002), Timothy Wilson talks about the processing that happens in the part of our brain that is not conscious: the *old brain*. The parts of our brain that are concerned with monitoring the environment and looking for danger are not immediately connected to the part of our brain that is conscious and thinking: our *new brain* (the cortex). So there is a lot of processing and decision-mak-ing that occurs that you are not even aware of.

"Sizing up" other people is one of those types of processing. The old brain is making sure you are safe, and it does that by quickly sizing up the situa-tion, the environment, and definitely the other people nearby. The old brain then decides whether you should flee the situation, have sex, or eat some-thing! It sounds crude and primitive, but that's what the old brain is—crude and primitive.

There is a lot of information to process, and all that processing is done in a split second. To process that quickly, the old brain takes a lot of shortcuts and makes broad generalizations.

The old brain is deciding if you should flee, eat, or have sex.

If we look at the refrigerator purchase scenario again, the old brain will size up the sales person. If the sales person is similar to you, then the decision (remember, all unconsciously) will be that you are safe and don't have to flee. This will also send signals to the mid brain (where emotions are processed) that this is someone you can trust.

If you find the sales person attractive, the old brain will be deciding whether this is a sex opportunity or not. Is this someone you might date and marry and have offspring with? The old brain is looking for opportunities to procreate. There doesn't seem to be any opportunity to eat—except that the refrigerator will hold food eventually!

After your old brain has finished its processing, you will either still be talking to the sales person, or you will have disregarded him and walked away. The final result of all this is that you are most influenced and persuaded by those whom you deem to be similar to you and attractive to you.

SIMILAR IS BETTER

SIMILARITY BUILDS RAPPORT. If we feel people are like us, we tend to like them more. We find it easier to like those we are similar to or those whom we perceive to share our background or values. It can even boil down to clothes. We like people who are dressed similarly to the way we are dressed. And we prefer to buy from people we like and are similar to.

VOTE FOR THE PERSON WITH THE BEST TEETH?

MY DAUGHTER WAS about six years old during a presidential election in the U.S. There were heated discussions at the dinner table about who was the best candidate. "I know who I would vote for," announced my daughter. "Who?" I asked. "The one with the best teeth." After the laughter died down,

I asked why she made that decision. "The one with the best teeth takes care of his teeth and that means he is responsible and will make the best president." Not a bad rule of thumb to follow. And, apparently, my daughter is not the only one using physical characteristics to decide who should be elected.

Efran and Patterson (1976) analyzed elections in Canada and found that attractive candidates received more than 2.5 times as many votes—despite the fact that 73 percent of voters said that attractiveness did not influence their vote. Cialdini (2007) reports on the large body of research that shows that people who are physically attractive are perceived to be smarter, more capable, and more intelligent. In addition, we just plain like people who are attractive.

A MATHEMATICAL FORMULA FOR ATTRACTIVENESS

IN A RESEARCH study by Gunes (2006), researchers took many different measurements of human faces. For example, they measured the distance from the top of the eyes to the bottom of the chin, the distance from the top of the eyes to the bottom of the nostrils, and so on. They compared these measurements to people's ratings of who was attractive. They found that most people agreed on who was attractive, and that those rated as attractive had certain proportions to their facial structures. Although attractiveness is affected by cultural and surface norms, such as clothing and hair, there does seem to be a mathematical basis to our decisions about who is attractive, and that basis seems to hold true across cultures.

Of course, we don't take a ruler to someone's face before we decide whether they are attractive or not. Our unconscious minds are able to process these mathematical proportions in the blink of an eye and send information to other parts of our brain, telling us that this person is attractive and we should pay attention.

What happens when an attractive person holds a can of beer or a power tool?

That old brain that is deciding who to trust, who is attractive, and who is similar to me also makes quick associations. If someone who is attractive or liked is paired or associated with something else, the attractiveness or liking "bleeds over" or rubs off on to the item that is close by. So, if an attractive person is holding a can of soda or beer, then the soda or beer becomes more interesting and attractive. There is an entire industry (called **product placement**) based on placing products in movies that attractive movie stars will then pick up and use as part of the movie scene.

If an attractive person is holding a can of beer or soda, then the beverage becomes more attractive.

Photo Credit: Katie Ricard

If you combine an attractive person with a sexual implication, well, that is even more compelling. That's when you have attention-getting, attraction, association, and sex—a pretty powerful combination.

Add an attractive person to sexual implication, and you get powerful attention and association for the power tool.

Unfortunate but true

Many of us will rebel against this idea that we are making decisions in the blink of an eye and that we are judging instantly whether someone is like us or whether they are attractive. Even worse, we are making our decisions about what to do and what to buy on such seemingly superficial and trivial characteristics. But it's true!

SNAG A CELEBRITY

NOT EVERYONE CAN get a celebrity to pose on the home page of his Web site (although Accenture got Tiger Woods, so it's possible). But celebrities draw attention and provide positive association.

If celebrity sightings aren't possible, then the next best idea is to use photos of attractive-looking people.

If you can't get a celebrity, photos of attractive people will provide positive persuasion and association.

www.bepresent.com

MAKE THEM LOOK LIKE ME

IN ORDER TO persuade people, the photos at a Web site need to match the target audience.

If the target audience is comprised of young, hip people, the site should use photos of young, hip people.

If the audience is comprised of the baby-boomer generation, the people in the photos should look like baby boomers. This prompts the old brain to say, "These people are like me. I should do what they are doing."

But sometimes instead of matching who the target audience is, it might be better to match who the audience wants to be. At the ThirdAge Web site, the page on beauty shows youthful photos. This prompts the old brain to say, "These people are really attractive. I'll do whatever it is they are doing."

Apparently, there aren't many people in the U.S. state or federal government

I tried to find some U.S. state and federal government sites with good and bad examples of using appropriate types and ages of people, and what a surprise I got. Very few U.S. state or federal sites use pictures at all! The California state Web site has photos of the governor and his wife, and a career site for baby boomers from the state of Tennessee includes some photos of baby boomers, so they've done a good job at working with the idea of similarity.

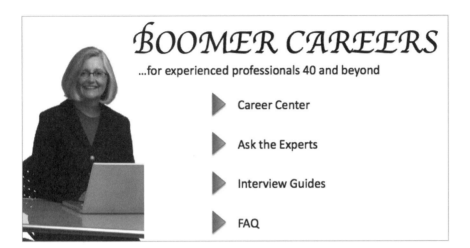

If your site is for a particular demographic, make sure the photos are similar.

But many government sites don't use pictures of people at all.

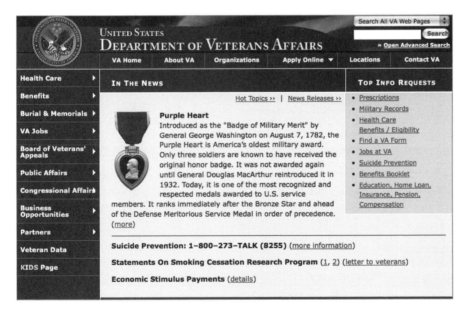

The Veterans Affairs Web site doesn't use any pictures.

This site for senior citizens doesn't use any pictures. Also, I have to ask, do they really think seniors can read type that small?

You get the picture... oh! There isn't a picture to get? The sites without any pictures miss out on the possible effects of similarity, attractiveness, and association.

NOT JUST PICTURES

ALTHOUGH PICTURES ARE very powerful (see Chapter 10), they are not the only way we make associations and decisions about similarities. Narratives can also convey similarity. If we read stories about a celebrity using a product, or we see someone who seems like us using a specific product or service, we will be persuaded to also use that product or service.

Date posted: December 28
Reviewed by: Susan, Maplewood

"The minute I saw my friend Margaret with this bag, I knew I had to have it. She walked into the restaurant where we were meeting for lunch, and looked so pulled together. She immediately dumped the contents of the bag on the table, and let me tell you, it was everything but the kitchen sink. I need a bag that will carry everything, work, clothes, phones, and still look somewhat fashionable. This was the bag. The size is very misleading. You really can fit everything in there. It's just amazing. I'll keep this one in rotation for awhile!"

- Type of user: Frequent Bag Changer
- Frequency of use: Monthly
- Occupation: Consultant
- Gender: Female

This person sounds like me, so I bet I'd like this product, too.

For the old brain, it's all about deciding to flee, eat, or have sex.

Don't underestimate the power of attractive people.

We are swayed most by those we think are similar to us.

Associating an object with a celebrity or an attractive person will make the object more attractive, too.

BOTTOM LINE

9

Afraid to Lose—How Fear of Loss
Trumps Our Anticipation of Victory

IMAGINE THAT YOU are a freelance graphic designer. You get a call from Sam Mullins, who owns the Mullins car dealership empire in your city. They have several large and successful car dealerships. He wants you to take over his account and provide all the graphic design work for all the car dealerships. It's a lucrative opportunity.

But it also turns out that Sam Mullins has been the enemy of your best friend for years. There is a feud between them that goes back to high school. Do you move forward with the meeting with Mullins and risk your friendship with your best friend? Or do you cancel the meeting, thereby keeping your friendship but giving up lots of potential and profitable work?

Let's walk through your reaction to this dilemma:

1 You would probably imagine a series of possible scenarios and the outcomes of each. Your new brain would be actively working.

2 If you continued to follow a rational new brain process, then next you would analyze each scenario and its consequence. You would conduct the equivalent of a cost-benefit analysis for each scenario in your new brain. You would analyze how much business might be gained from the new client. You would analyze the likelihood of really ruining your friendship and analyze the benefits that your relationship gives you. You would consider the consequences of losing that relationship.

3 You would continue to create and imagine these scenarios, and you could continue to analyze the cost-benefits. This process would take a long time. You might not even reach a decision. It might be too complicated to remember all the scenarios, all their outcomes, and all the cost-benefit analyses. You might lose track and get distracted.

In reality, this is not how you make such decisions. Here is what really happens:

1 It is true that you would start with imagining a series of possible scenarios. This happens visually. Little "movies" play in your new brain as you imagine what might happen.

2 As each movie plays in your new brain, your mid brain and your old brain react. You will have "gut" feelings. Some of the movies will make you feel good and others will make you feel bad. This is your mid brain that is active.

3 The movies that make you feel bad will be picked up by the old brain. The old brain will sense threat, or danger to your well being, and will send out alarm signals telling your mid brain and new brain that a particular movie is dangerous and should be avoided. Of course, the mid brain and old brain activity is not under conscious control or even conscious monitoring. But the old brain signal of danger, and the mid brain reaction of not liking the movie, will eventually be picked up by the new brain, and the new brain will "decide" to reject that particular action and to look for another alternative.

This automatic signaling from the old brain and mid brain protects you from losing something. It's also an efficiency measure, since you will end up with a smaller set of alternatives to decide among.

> *Our old brain and mid brain react quickly to choices and reduce our alternatives based on minimizing loss.*

IS IT A SNAKE?

THE OLD BRAIN, mid brain, and new brain all work together. Here is an example that is often used.

Have you ever been walking in the woods and you are suddenly startled by something on the path ahead of you? Before you can think what is happening you have jumped back, your heart is racing, your adrenaline is flowing. Is it a snake? Did you see a snake? Oh, you realize, it is just a stick that kind of looks like a snake. Your heart rate returns to normal and you continue on your way.

What just happened?

Remember when we talked about the amygdala? The amygdala (there are two of them, one in the right half of your brain and one in the left half) is where emotions are processed. There are two pathways in and out of the amygdala:

1. One comes from the new brain.
2. The other is a direct path from the senses.

LeDoux's (1996) and Phelps (2005) both studied the research on the amygdala. From their work, the theory has emerged that the two pathways in and out of the amygdala work together. Information from the senses will reach the amygdala very quickly, but the amygdala isn't capable of processing sensory detail. The amygdala will not "see" the details of what your eyes saw. So the information will only be a vague image or idea. Your eyes are seeing something, and that sensory information is coming through that "low road" pathway to your amygdala—the path that goes directly from the senses to the mid brain. The amygdala can't process visual information the way the new brain can, so it doesn't see the stick clearly. It only registers something that "kind of maybe" looks like a snake, but that is enough to have the mid brain talk to the old brain and set the alarm bells ringing. You react, jump back, and have an entire chemical and hormonal reaction that prepares you to fight the snake or flee from it. While all that is going on, the visual part of the new brain has now analyzed the "snake" and realized that it is a stick. That took longer than the automatic old brain and mid brain reactions, so your body had its automatic reaction before the new brain kicked in with the analysis.

> *There are two pathways for sensory information into our brains: A fast one through the amygdala and a slower more thorough one through the new brain.*

FEARING A BLUE SQUARE

IF I ASK you where you were and what you were doing on July 16, 2002, chances are you won't be able to remember. But if I ask you where you were and what you were doing on September 11, 2001, you will be able to tell me in minute detail where you were and what you were doing. If you are an American and over 40 years old, I can ask you the same question about where you were and what you were doing when the space shuttle Challenger exploded and everyone on board was killed, including a teacher. You can probably remember details from that date. And if you are over 55 years old, you can probably tell me where you were and what you were doing when President John F. Kennedy was shot.

How is it possible that you can remember these events from long ago, and yet you've forgotten most details from all the other days?

It's because of the amygdala. The amygdala codes any events that produce emotional reactions. The result is that these emotional events are remembered better than events that were not connected with strong emotions.

Phelps (2005) describes experiments in which participants were shown a blue square while simultaneously receiving a mild shock. When we are aroused or upset, our skin emits a tiny amount of sweat. It's not enough for anyone to notice, but a sensor on the skin will pick it up as an increase in the **skin conductance response (SCR)**. When the participants in Phelps' experiment received the mild shock, their SCR increased. Before too long, experimenters needed only to show the blue square to elicit an increase in SCR. When researchers scanned the brains of the participants, they also saw their amygdala light up when they were shown blue squares—supporting the notion that simply imagining a fearful event is enough to activate the amygdala.

The **hippocampus** is involved in memory and is located directly next to the amygdala in the mid brain. The amygdala identifies that something should be feared, and the hippocampus connects that feeling to conscious cognitive experience and memory in the new brain. When we are afraid, we are aroused, and when we are aroused, we remember better. (Actually, it's really the opposite. When we are aroused, we forget less quickly, so that's kind of the same thing as remembering better.)

When we are emotionally aroused, whether negatively or positively, we forget the event less quickly, which means we encode it into our long-term memory more effectively.

YOUR UNCONSCIOUS IS SMARTER THAN YOU THINK

THESE EMOTIONAL RESPONSES can occur without us being aware of them. The amygdala responds to the emotional significance of what is going on around us long before it responds to cognitive awareness. In a research study, Whalen (1998) showed faces with emotions, such as fear, to participants so quickly that they weren't even aware that they had seen anything. But the fMRI brain scan revealed that their amygdala had lit up. The amygdala is deciding what is important and what we should pay attention to—and remember, we're not aware of it. The amygdala is especially tuned into situations in which we should be afraid of losing. We are programmed to pay attention to, and to avoid, loss.

The best research study on the unconscious fear of losing was conducted by Bechara and others (1997). Participants played a gambling game with decks of cards. Each person received $2,000 of money that he or she knew wasn't real (but it was designed to look real in an effort to fool their unconscious). They were told that the goal was to lose as little of the $2,000 as possible, and to try to make as much over the $2,000 as possible. There were four decks of cards on the table. The participants turned over a card from any of the four decks, one card at a time. They continued turning over a card from the deck of their choice until the experimenter told them to stop. They didn't know when the game would end. The participants were told that every time they turned over a card, they earned money. They were also told that sometimes when they turned over a card, they earned money but also *lost* money (by paying it to the experimenter).

At the beginning of the game, participants didn't know how much money they would gain or lose for any particular card. They also didn't know if the four decks were the same or if they were different. They discovered how much they earned or lost only *after* a card was turned over. They weren't given any information about how they were doing (in other words, there was no tally they could look at). They also weren't allowed to keep a tally themselves on paper or take notes of any kind.

The participants didn't know any of the rules of the gambling game:

- If they turned over any card in decks A or B, they earned $100. If they turned over any card in decks C and D, they earned only $50.

- Some cards in decks A and B also required participants to pay the experimenter a lot of money, sometimes as much as $1,250. Some cards in decks C and D also required participants to pay the experimenter, but the amount they had to pay was only an average of $100.

- Over the course of the game, decks A and B produced net losses if participants continued using them. Continued use of decks C and D rewarded participants with net gains.

- The rules of the game never changed. Although participants didn't know this, the game ended after 100 cards had been "played" (turned over).

So what happened? Did they figure out the rules and use some decks more than others?

Most participants started by trying all four decks. At first, they gravitated toward decks A and B because those decks paid out $100 per turn. But after about 30 turns, most turned to decks C and D. They then continued turning cards in decks C and D until the game ended.

During the study, the experimenter stopped the game several times to ask participants about the decks. The participants were connected to a skin conductance sensor to measure their SCRs. Their SCR readings were elevated when they played decks A and B (the "dangerous" decks) long before participants consciously realized that A and B were dangerous. When the participants played decks A and B, their SCRs increased even before they touched the cards in the decks. Their SCRs increased when they *thought* about using decks A and B.

Eventually, participants said they had a "hunch" that decks C and D were better, but the SCR shows that the old brain figured this out long before the new brain "got" it. By the end of the game, most participants had more than a hunch and could articulate the difference in the two decks, but a full 30 percent of the participants couldn't explain why they preferred decks C and D. They said they just thought those decks were better.

Again, our mid brains and old brains are watching out for us and are particularly sensitive to the prospect of losing. They will signal an alarm long before the conscious mind is aware that anything is wrong.

One of the most interesting results of this study was the spike in skin conductance (SCR) before participants were aware of differences in the decks. Their bodies and their unconscious minds knew what was happening before their conscious minds knew.

Our old and mid brains know what is going on before our new brain does.

WHAT ARE WE AFRAID OF?

SO WHAT IS it we are afraid of losing, anyway? It's all sorts of things. We're most afraid of losing what we already have. In the example at the beginning of the chapter, where you weighed the prospect of losing a friendship with the potential of gaining a new client, it is most likely that you will give up the potential work to hold on to the friendship because you already have the friendship. (Remember the adage, "A bird in the hand is worth two in the bush.")

LOSING WHAT YOU ALMOST HAVE

BARRY SCHWARTZ (2004) researched people buying cars. Participants test-drove cars with all the options.

- In one condition, they were shown the price of the car with all the options. If they said the price was too expensive, they then were asked to take away the options in an effort to reduce the price.

- In another condition, they were shown the base price of the car (without options) along with a description and price of each option. They were asked to select which options they wanted to add, increasing the price with each option.

We will spend more money in the first condition. The theory is that we have experienced the car in its entirety and will be reluctant to lose what we, in some sense, feel we already have.

SUBTRACT, DON'T ADD

THE WEB SITE that follows uses the same principle discussed in the previous section. The model of computer you are configuring in this example already has the better processor. It is "included in price." If you want to spend less money, then you choose a lesser processor and subtract money. This uses the **Fear of Losing principle**—we're reluctant to take away or subtract items. This means we'll spend more money than if we had started with a lower-end (and less expensive) processor and were asked to spend more money to get a better model.

Select My Processor:

- ⦿ Intel Duo T8300 – Included in Price
- ◎ Intel Core2 Duo – Subtract $135.00
- ◎ Intel Pentium Core Duo – Subtract $225.00
- ◎ Intel Celeron 550 – Subtract $275.00   Next>

If the choices subtract, rather than add, then they are using the Fear of Losing principle.

In order to entice us to spend more money, it's even better if the Web site shows us the entire package (preferably in a compelling photo or, even better, a video.) With photos and video, we can see and almost feel all the options, hear the rich sound of the speakers, or be wowed by the large screen. Then if we feel we can't afford the entire package, we have to face the idea of taking away options—an idea we don't necessarily like. If we experience the entire package, we will be even more reluctant to take something away.

IS IT 90 PERCENT GOOD
OR 10 PERCENT BAD?

DAMASIO (1994) POINTED out that we have such an automatic fear of losing, that even the way things are phrased can be important. He cited research in the medical field showing that when patients are told "if you undergo this medical treatment, you have a 90 percent chance of living," patients choose the treatment. If, however, patients are told "if you undergo this medical treatment, you have a 10 percent chance of *dying*," patients are much less likely to choose the treatment.

So even the way you word something can trigger the fear of losing.

A 90% chance of success is better than saying 10% chance of failing.

> **This new sales system will give you a 90% chance of success!**
> **It's GUARANTEED!**

FEAR OF LOSING PRIVACY

THERE ARE MANY ways that fear of losing can be triggered while online. Certainly the fear of losing privacy can stop us from taking action at a Web site. We might be afraid that by filling out a form that includes our personal information, someone will use that information to start marketing new products to us.

A friend told me about a fun IQ test that someone sent her. She answered the first five questions, and then the site asked two personal questions, one of which was her birthday. She suspected the site was asking her for personal information, so she used a random birthday.

As covered in Chapter 3, research showed that we were more willing to fill out a form *after* we had received useful information. That is one way that Web sites can alleviate the fear of losing.

FEAR OF LOSING SECURITY

ALTHOUGH MOST YOUNG people are not afraid of purchasing items on the Internet, many older individuals (who have not grown up online and aren't as familiar with the technology) report that they are afraid to purchase items online because they fear identity theft. In this case, their fear of losing might prevent them from taking an action to purchase.

In fact, some Web sites can make a compelling call to action by combining fear of losing with other techniques, such as telling stories.

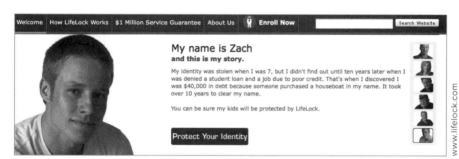

Fear of losing security is very motivating.

www.lifelock.com

We are programmed to notice and pay attention to situations that might result in our fear of losing.

Fear of losing motivates us more than the opportunity to win.

Our bodies and our unconscious will pick up on possible loss situations faster than our conscious mind picks up on them.

If an event is associated with emotion, we will remember it better.

Even subtle wording can affect our response.

BOTTOM LINE

10

**Using Pictures and Stories—
the Best Way to Talk to Our
Unconscious Minds**

Photo Credit: Katie Ricard

I LIKE TO TEACH seminars and give talks. I've been doing public speaking for many years. One of the interesting things I've noticed is the effect on the audience of the words, "Let me tell you a story." It's as though I said, "Once upon a time." Every time I say, "Let me tell you a story," everyone looks up at me. Their eyes get big, their eyebrows go up, and I have their total attention.

When we hear a story, we give the storyteller all of our attention. A good story communicates information thoroughly and commits the information to memory.

> **If you want to get and hold someone's attention, tell a story.**

WHAT IS A STORY?

IF YOU SEARCH on "What is a story" in Google, you will get several sites with various definitions. Wikipedia says: "A narrative or story is a construct created in a suitable format (written, spoken, poetry, prose, images, song, theater, or dance) that describes a sequence of fictional or non-fictional events."

In some definitions a narrative is always fictional, and in other definitions a narrative is just another word for a story. For our purposes here, I will use narrative and story as synonyms. And the definition I'll use is this: a description of a character or characters and a relating of what happens to the characters over time (past or future). The character might be you or someone you know, or a fictitious person, or an animal. The character could be your car or your computer.

EVERYONE IS A STORYTELLER

WHEN WE HEAR the word "storyteller," we often think of some overly dramatic person telling a story to children using different voices. But we are all storytellers. Think about your communication with other people throughout a typical day. You wake up in the morning and tell your family about a dream you had (story). At work you tell a coworker about what happened at the new product's design meeting the day before (story). At lunch you tell your friend about a family reunion you have coming up and your plans to take time off to go to it (story). After work you speak with your neighbor about the dog you encountered while you were on your evening walk (story). At dinner you describe to your family the odd sounds the car made repeatedly while you were driving home from work (story). And on and on.

When you think about it, you realize that most of the communication we do in our daily lives is in the form of a story. Yet we rarely stop and think about stories and storytelling. Storytelling is so ubiquitous that we don't even realize we are doing it.

If someone at work suggested you attend a workshop on how to communicate clearly at work, you might be interested. But how many of us would scoff if it were suggested that we attend a workshop on storytelling? It's interesting how unaware and unappreciative we are of the major way we communicate.

> *"A well-told story conveys great quantities of information in relatively few words in a format that is easily assimilated by the listener or viewer." Nahum Gershon*

YOUR BRAIN NATURALLY CHUNKS

STORIES ARE AN excellent way for us to process and store information. A story contains a large amount of information in digestible chunks. Stories allow us to break down events into smaller units so that we can better understand the information being communicated. Psychologists call this chunking of parts of a story **event structure perception**.

Research by Nicole Speer (2007) showed the brain activity associated with event structure perception. Participants read narratives about everyday activities, and she measured their brain activity using fMRI. The fMRI pictures showed a burst of activity, then a pause, then another burst, then another pause, and so on. The brain was processing the story in chunks.

The participants were invited back a few days later to reread these same narratives, this time without the fMRI scan. Instead, they were asked to mark the narrative where they thought one chunk in the story ended and another began.

When Speer compared the brain pictures to the chunking the participants gave, she found that these patterns of activity and pause matched. These beginning and end points are called **event boundaries**. The event boundaries occur when there is a transition in the story, such as a change in location or a different character.

The stories that Nicole Speer used in her research were stories about everyday events. The theory is that our brains are wired to process the world around us as a story.

I FEEL YOUR PAIN

STORIES INVOLVE MANY parts of the brain. When we are reading or listening to a story, there are many parts of our brain that are active, including the following parts of the new brain:

- The auditory part of the new brain that deciphers sound (if the story is being told)

- Vision and text processing (if the story is being read)

- All of the visual parts of the brain (as we imagine the characters in the story)

- And, often, the emotional part of the mid brain

A story not only conveys information, but it also allows us to feel what the character in the story feels. Tania Singer's research on empathy (Singer, 2004) studied the parts of the brain that react to pain.

First, she used fMRI scans to see what parts of the brain were active when the participants experienced pain. She discovered that there were some parts of the brain that processed where the pain came from and how intense the pain really was. Other parts of the brain separately processed how unpleasant the pain felt and how much the pain bothered the person feeling it.

Then she asked participants to read stories about people experiencing pain. When participants read stories about someone in pain, the parts of the brain that processed where the pain came from and how intense it was were not active—but the other areas that processed how unpleasant the pain was *were* active.

When we read or hear a story, our brains are partly reacting as though we are experiencing the story ourselves.

A PICTURE IS WORTH....

WHEN WE THINK about a story (or actually when we think about anything), we think in pictures and visual images.

> *"Images are the main content of our thoughts regardless of the sensory modality in which they are generated and regardless of whether they are about a thing or a process involving things, or about words or other symbols." Antonio Damasio*

The visual part of the brain takes up half of the brain processing power. An enormous amount of the new brain is devoted to processing visual images. So it shouldn't be a surprise that we remember things we have seen visually better than anything else. In fact, there is a special name for this. It's called **pictorial superiority effect (PSE)**.

Research from the 1960s to the present (Brady, 2008) confirms that human memory for visual information is vast. People can remember more than 2,500 pictures with 90 percent accuracy. In his book *Brain Rules*, John J. Medina reviews research from the 1960s that shows that we can remember pictures a year later (accuracy rate is 63 percent). In one study, individuals could remember the pictures decades later. This is in contrast to information that we read or hear. We remember only 10 percent of what we hear or read (without pictures).

IT ALL TURNS INTO PICTURES

WHEN WE READ, we are actually processing pictures—we break the words into letters and the letters into small patterns and shapes. We process those shapes in our new brain into words, and then process the meaning of the words, and then turn the words and phrases into pictures. Whew! That's a lot of processing! And what do we end up with? Pictures in our brains!

Our brains are built to process pictures, and we think in pictures, so presenting information as pictures is the most efficient way to present information to people. From an evolutionary standpoint, we were processing visual images (our environment around us) for millions of years before we encountered text (a mere few thousand years at most).

And if you remember from Chapter 6, the old brain is always scanning the environment to see what has changed and what might signal danger or food or sex. The old brain doesn't "pick up" text information in this way. It pays attention to visual images.

PUTTING IT ALL TOGETHER

SO IF YOU combine the fact that we process information as stories, we turn stories we hear into mental images, and that PSE is real, you realize that stories and pictures at Web sites are the most powerful ways to get and hold our attention and persuade us to take action.

In several chapters in this book, we've seen that pictures and stories can be compelling. When used together at a Web site, they are almost irresistible.

This Web site combines pictures of maps and stories of exciting events. It's very powerful and effective.

Lifelock.com makes great use of photos and stories. Notice in the following example that the story also involves danger, which gets the attention of the old brain. A scary photo to accompany the story about thieves would be even better, but Lifelock uses many stories and photos, and together they make for a compelling home page.

A picture of a person, combined with a compelling story. Notice the words, "this is my story," and the first word of the story is "thieves." Very attention-getting.

What a great name for a Web site: StoryCorps. And they use both pictures and stories to communicate.

BOTTOM LINE

We are programmed to think in stories. Web sites with stories will grab our attention.

Using the word "story" will grab our attention.

We pay attention to and remember pictures better than words.

Combining pictures and stories together is an unbeatable combination to grab our attention, hold our attention, and help us remember.

11

We're Social Animals—Finding the Next Big Thing by Making It Social

Photo Credit: Katie Ricard

THE YEAR WAS 2000, and I was on the phone with a client from Motorola. Instead of talking about the project at hand, we found ourselves discussing cell phones. "I headed up the original team to invent the cell phone, you know," he told me. I was impressed. "Yep," he said, "my team invented the cell phone and then we shelved the entire project for years."

"Why?" I asked. "Why didn't you bring it to market right away?" He answered, "Well, we thought we'd only be making about 10 of them. Not much of a market."

"Ten of them? Why did you think that?" I asked.

He replied, "We figured each head of state for major nations would have one. You know, the President of the United States, the head guy in Russia, and so on. We thought they'd use it to prevent a world war. I had no idea people would use it to call home before leaving work to see if they should pick up milk!"

CAUGHT BY OUR OWN SHORTSIGHTEDNESS

THIS IS WHAT always happens. When we are thinking about new ways to use technology, we are stuck in our "present" way of thinking. The new, actual ways that technology will be used in the future don't even occur to us. But there is one route out of this shortsightedness. And that is to think about being social.

We are social animals. Being human means being social. It is built into our brains and evolution to live together with others and to be very influenced by our "pack" or group. History shows us that whatever technology there is, we will find a way to use it to communicate—to make it social.

FROM THE PRINTING PRESS TO FACEBOOK

IF YOU SPEND some time thinking back on technology, you will see that there are many instances of how we have co-opted technology to use it as a means to be social and to communicate.

The printing press allowed people to communicate via the written word in a way that was much faster. Before the printing press, each book had to be copied by hand, a task that sometimes took years. The printing press reduced that time to days and, in some instances, only hours. That allowed people to communicate quickly. (Remember that much of the original printing was not in the form of long books; it was in the form of short pamphlets or even one-page "bills," such as bulletins.) The printing press was truly a form of mass communication.

When the first telephones were being developed, they were viewed as an updated version of the telegraph. There was no plan to put telephones in homes. The assumption was that telephones would be in the telegraph offices and be used to convey messages from telegraph office to telegraph office (and from there, the message would be written out and delivered).

Even when the use of telephones expanded, they were used first in businesses, not homes. The inventors and initial manufacturers simply didn't conceive of telephones in homes.

But consumers pushed the demand for technology that would help them communicate and help them be social. Consumers wanted telephones in their homes. We will always push the envelope to bend the available technology to purposes that extend and improve our communication and the opportunity to be social.

THE REAL REASON THE INTERNET WAS STARTED

IF YOU LOOK up online descriptions of the history of the Internet, you will find a lot of articles about packet switching and other technologies associated with the Internet. But the truth is, the history of the Internet is actually founded in social needs and our collective frustration with machines that made communication slow and cumbersome.

J.C.R. Licklider was appointed as head of the United State's Department of Defense Advanced Research Projects Agency in 1962. (It was called ARPA then. Now it's called DARPA.) It's true that he had been thinking about networks for a few years. But it was his frustration at having to use three different terminals that led to the development of the Internet.

At DARPA, Licklider had formed an informal group to study computer research. The group was dispersed at different organizations, and each organization had its own computer system, so he had three different screens, each connected to a different terminal. For those readers who are too young to remember this, in the "old days," if you wanted to work on a computer system, you had to have that system's terminal installed in your office.

Each of the three terminals had its own screen connected to a separate system, and each system had a different set of commands. If he was talking to someone at Berkeley on one terminal and he wanted to talk to someone at

MIT, he had to get up from one terminal and log into another terminal, using a different set of commands on that one, and so on. He became frustrated with how difficult it was to communicate. He thought to himself, "It should work over one network." And then he began the work that made the one-network concept a reality. He wanted ARPA scientists to be able to communicate more effectively over a computer network.

EISENHOWER SIGNS THE CIVIL RIGHTS ACT, CASSIUS CLAY WINS A GOLD MEDAL IN BOXING, AND ...

As early as 1960 Licklider wrote about "A network of such [computers], connected to one another by wide-band communication lines [which provided] the functions of present-day libraries together with anticipated advances in information storage and retrieval and [other] symbiotic functions." (Licklider, 1960)

Today, the Internet is used for a wide variety of purposes. Certainly businesses use it to sell products and services. But it was initially used to communicate, and it has retained that use over time.

Email has become one of the most frequently used applications of computers. We use instant messaging both at work and at home.

It was just a matter of time before special Web sites would arrive whose purpose was linking people together. It was inevitable that this would happen, because humans will always take technology and find a way to use it to help them be social.

Early "social networking" Web sites included Classmates.com (started in 1995) and Epinions.com (started in 1999). Then MySpace came along in 2003. And LinkedIn targeted the business community (started in 2003).

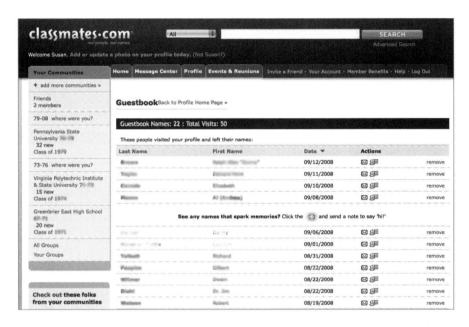

Classmates.com was one of the first social networking Web sites.

Epinions was another early social networking site.

After Classmates. com and epinions, next came MySpace.

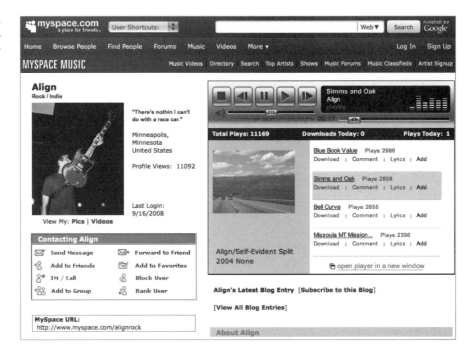

And then the business community decided to go social with LinkedIn.

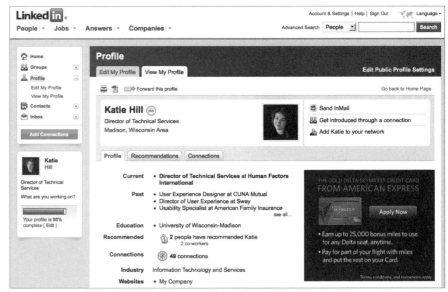

Facebook began as a social networking site for college students in 2004, but, as of the writing of this book, Facebook has taken prominence as the social networking site for high school students, college students, and adults. Along came Twitter in 2006, helping us keep in touch with our social networks on the Internet and via text messages on our cell phones.

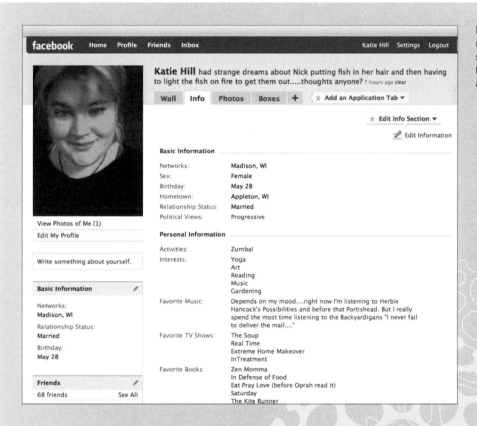

Facebook is not just for high school and college students anymore.

Twitter is all about short messages you can broadcast and read on the Internet or via text messages on your phone.

@warrenss no, just saw your tweet, http://is.gd/2xXn , and the way you phrased, wasn't sure if that meant anything more than following us 01:38 PM September 12, 2008 from twhirl in reply to warrenss

@warrenss curious, how do you 'use' us? 10:02 AM September 12, 2008 from twhirl in reply to warrenss

Footage from St. Paul -- In Praise of Sarah Palin and Moose at the Republican Convention: http://is.gd/2vzD 04:26 PM September 11, 2008 from twhirl

SEDC Audit Reveals Fraud: http://is.gd/Rhw 04:52 PM September 10, 2008 from twhirl

RNC mobile photo -- NPR breaking down http://is.gd/2eL9 09:32 PM September 04, 2008 from twitterfeed

@Smiff chatted, he was indeed kidding 09:15 PM September 04, 2008 from twitterrific in reply to Smiff

@Smiff he said alt. delegate so i guess so. will confirm hopefully if we can find and chat with him now 08:32 PM September 04, 2008 from twhirl in reply to Smiff

Protesters being carried out, aka "ground noise and static" says McCain 07:25 PM September 04, 2008 from twhirl

RNC mobile photo -- 'Make Noise' http://is.gd/2exf 07:02 PM September 04, 2008 from twitterfeed

Just bumped into author Jeremy Scahill, apparently he's an alternate delegate from North Dakota 06:35 PM September 04, 2008 from twitterrific

Updates   1,390

Following

MASS INTERPERSONAL COMMUNICATION

SOCIAL NETWORKING SITES allow information to spread very quickly as they move from person to person, "virally."

Social networking sites are changing the way we communicate about everything.

Come to Odie's FIRST birthday party!!!

Saturday, September 20, 2008
2:30 PM
144 Main Street
Madison, WI
55443

RSVP Regrets only

All presents welcome!

YouTube allows anyone, anywhere there is an Internet connection, to upload a video they create. After that, who knows who will be watching it. When my son had his wisdom teeth pulled, I drove him home from the surgery. While we were driving home, he used his digital camera to make a movie of himself under the influence of the dental drugs. Later that day I went to my local grocery store to pick up some soft food for him to eat. Imagine my surprise when someone stopped me in the store and said how funny they thought my son's video was from the wisdom teeth surgery. My son had uploaded the video to YouTube where it was being virally spread all around—in a matter of hours. I just checked, and the video has been watched over 700 times and even has a five-star rating!

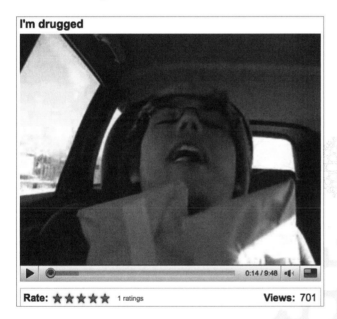

Videos spread virally, too.

When my daughter had her 17th birthday party, she didn't send paper invitations, and she didn't call her friends on the phone—she just sent out invitations via Facebook.

Hallmark beware—does anyone buy party invitations anymore?

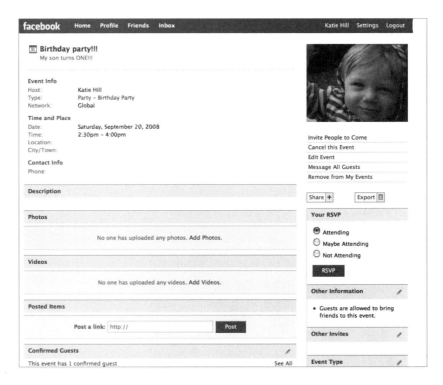

When political candidates want to invite people to an event, or raise money, they send out Facebook invites.

The new way to get people involved is to create events on Facebook and then invite everyone.

MASS INTERPERSONAL PERSUASION (MIP)

B. J. FOGG (2008) has coined **MIP** (**Mass Interpersonal Persuasion**). This is a combination of mass media and persuasion techniques. He uses Facebook as an example of this new technology, especially the use of third-party applications.

One of those third-party applications is iLike, a social networking site that allows members to share music and information about music. iLike also sells CDs, concert tickets, and so on. iLike launched in October of 2006 and by June of 2007, it had three million members. A million members joined every month, and at this writing, membership is 30 million. Such is the power of being social.

Fogg and Eckles (2007) described what they called the "**behavior chain**" for enticing us to participate online at social networking sites. They describe three phases:

1. Phase 1 is **Discovery**. We learn about the service and visit the site.

2. Phase 2 is **Superficial Involvement**. We try out the service and get started.

3. Phase 3 is **True Commitment**. We create content, use the site, involve others, and stay active and loyal.

A successful online social site must pay attention to each phase and decide how to get us to take action on each phase. For example, how is it that we learn about the service and decide to visit the site? What does the site do to entice us to try it out once we get there? Is there compelling content that we can create once we're there? Is the site using viral communication so that we will be so excited by what we created that we will want to share it with others?

If the site wants to be as successful as iLike, it needs to focus on these target behaviors.

HOW TO BE PERSUASIVE ONLINE

WEIKSNER, FOGG, AND LIU (2008) analyzed the types of persuasion used in Facebook applications. They identified that popular third-party applications (such as Poke, Superwall, and Hotness) use the basic principles of reciprocity, social validation, and similarity to promote themselves and cause a viral spread. For example, if you give me a "poke" on Facebook, then I may feel the need to give you a return poke or give you something back. All the principles and ideas in this book can be used on social networking sites.

THE NEXT BIG THING

I DON'T KNOW what the next big thing online will be. I wish I did know. Then I could create it and make a lot of money and retire. But I do know that the next big thing will involve something social. Because it always does.

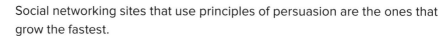

BOTTOM LINE

We are social animals. We will always figure out a way to use whatever technology is there to communicate and be social.

Social networking sites that use principles of persuasion are the ones that grow the fastest.

If you want to be the next big thing, figure out how to use a new technology in a social way.

Appendix

BIBLIOGRAPHY

Bargh, John A., Mark Chen, Lara Burrows. 1996. Automaticity of social behavior: Direct effects of trait construct and stereotype. *Journal of Personality and Social Psychology* Vol 71(2), 230-244.

Bechara, A., H. Damasio, D. Tranel, and A.R. Damasio. 1997. Deciding advantageously before knowing advantageous strategy. *Science.* 275, 1293-1295.

Brady, T.F., T. Konkle, G.A. Alvarez, and A. Oliva. 2008. Visual long-term memory has a massive storage capacity for object details. *Proceedings of the National Academy of Sciences, USA.* Vol. 105(38), 14325-14329.

Cialdini, R.B. 2007. *The Psychology of Influence.* New York: Harper Collins.

Cialdini, R.B., J.E. Vincent, S.K. Lewis, J. Catalan, D. Wheeler, B.L. Darby. 1975. A reciprocal concessions procedure for inducing compliance: The door-in-the-face technique. *Journal of Personality and Social Psychology.* 31:206-215.

Damasio, Antonio. 1994. *Descartes' Error.* New York: Penguin.

Deutsch, Morton, and Harold B. Gerard. 1955. A study of normative and informational social influences upon individual judgment. *The Journal of Abnormal and Social Psychology.* Vol 51(3), 629-636.

De Vries, Peter and Ad Pruyn. 2007. Source Salience and the Persuasiveness of Peer Recommendations: The Mediating Role of Social Trust. In *Persuasive Technology, Second International Conference on Persuasive Technology.* New York: Springer.

Dijksterhuis, A and Z. van Olden. 2005. On the benefits of thinking unconsciously: Unconscious thought can increase post-choice satisfaction. *Journal of Experimental and Social Psychology.* Vol 42(5), 627-631.

Efran, M.G. and E.W.J. Patterson. 1976. Voters vote beautiful: The effect of physical appearance on a national election. *Canadian Journal of Behavioural Science.* Vol 6(4), 352-356.

Felfernig, A., G. Friedrich, B. Gula, M. Hitz, T. Kruggel, G. Leitner, R. Melcher, D. Riepan, S. Strauss, E. Teppan, and O. Vitouch. 2007. Persuasive recommendation: Serial position effects in knowledge-based recommender systems. In *Persuasive Technology, Second International Conference on Persuasive Technology.* New York: Springer.

Fogg, B.J., 2008. Mass interpersonal persuasion: An early view of a new phenomenon. In *Persuasive Technology, Third International Conference on Persuasive Technology.* New York: Springer.

Freedman, Jonathan L. and Scott C. Fraser. 1966. Compliance without pressure: The foot-in-the-door technique. *Journal of Personality and Social Psychology.* Vol 4(2), 195-202.

Fogg, B.J. and D. Eckles. 2007. The Behavior Chain for Online Participation: How Successful Web Services Structure Persuasion In Persuasive Technology, Second International Conference on Persuasive Technology. New York: Springer.

Gamberini, Luciano, Giovanni Petrucci, Andrea Spoto, Anna Spagnolli. 2007. Embedded persuasive strategies to obtain visitors' data: Comparing reward and reciprocity in an amateur, knowledge-based website. In *Persuasive Technology, Second International Conference on Persuasive Technology.* New York: Springer.

Gunes, Hatice and Massimo Piccardi. 2006. Assessing facial beauty through proportion analysis by image processing and supervised learning. *International Journal of Human-Computer Studies.* Vol 64(12), 1184-1199.

Hassin, Ran R. 2005. Nonconscious control and implicit working memory. In *The New Unconscious,* edited by R.R. Hassin, J.S. Uleman and A. Bargh. New York: Oxford University Press.

Heinrich, J.R., S. Boyd, S. Bowles, C. Camerer. E. Fehr, and R. McElreath. 2001. Cooperation, reciprocity and punishment in fifteen small-scale societies. *American Economic Review.* May 2001.

Iyengar, Sheena S. and Mark R. Lepper. 2000. When choice is demotivating: Can one desire too much of a good thing?. *Journal of Personality and Social Psychology.* 79: 995-1006.

Kunz, P.R. and M. Woolcott. 1976. Season's Greetings: From my status to yours. *Social Science Research.* 5:269-278.

Latane, Bibb, and John M. Darley. 1970. *The Unresponsive Bystander*: *Why Doesn't He Help?* Upper Saddle River, NJ: Prentice Hall.

Latane, Bibb, and John M. Darley. 1968. Group inhibition of bystander intervention in emergencies. *Journal of Personality and Social Psychology.* Vol 10(3), 215-221.

Leakey, R.E., and R. Lewin. 1978. *People of the lake: Mankind and its beginnings.* New York: Anchor Press.

LeDoux, Joseph. 1996. *The Emotional Brain.* New York: Simon and Schuster.

Lewicki, P., T. Hill, and E. Bizot. 1988. Acquisition of procedural knowledge about a pattern of stimuli that cannot be articulated. *Cognitive Psychology.* 20:24-37.

Licklider, J.C.R. 1960. Man-Computer Symbiosis. *IRE Transactions on Human Factors in Electronics*. HFE-1:4-11.

Markey, P.M. 2000. Bystander intervention in computer-mediated communication. *Computers in Human Behavior*. Vol 16(2), 183-188.

McClure, S.M., D.I. Laibson, G. Loewenstein, and J.D. Cohen. 2004. Separate neural systems value immediate and delayed monetary rewards. *Science*. Vol 306 (5695), 503-507.

Medina, John. *Brain Rules*. Seattle: Pear Press, 2008.

New York Times. 1995. Reviving Kitty Genovese Case, and Its Passions. July 25, article by Joe Saxton.

Phelps, Elizabeth. 2005. The intersection of emotion and cognition: The relation between the human amygdala and cognitive awareness. In *The New Unconscious*, edited by R.R. Hassin, J.S. Uleman, and J.A. Bargh. New York: Oxford University Press.

Regan, Dennis T. 1971. Effects of a favor and liking on Compliance. *Journal of Experimental and Social Psychology*. Vol 7(6), 627-639.

Schwartz, Barry. 2004. *The Paradox of Choice*. New York: Harper Collins.

Singer, T., B. Seymour, J. O'Doherty, H. Kaube, J.D. Dolan, and C. Frith. 2004. Empathy for pain involves the affective but not sensory component of pain. *Science*. 303: 1157-1162.

Speer, Nicole K., Jeffrey M. Zacks and Jeremy R. Reynolds. 2007. Human brain activity time-locked to narrative event boundaries. *Psychological Science*. Vol 18(5), 449-455.

Weiksner, G. Michael, B.J. Fogg, and Xiangxin Liu. 2008. Six patterns for persuasion in online social networks. In *Persuasive Technology, Third International Conference on Persuasive Technology*. New York: Springer.

Whalen P.J., S.L. Rauch, N.L. Etcoff, S.C. McInerney, M. Lee, M.A. Jenike. 1998. Masked presentations of emotional facial expressions modulate amygdala activity without explicit knowledge. *Journal of Neuroscience*. 18: 411-418.

Wilson, Timothy D. and D. Kraft. 1993. Why do I love thee? Effects of repeated introspections on attitudes toward the relationship. *Personality and Social Psychology Bulletin*, 19: 409-418.

Wilson, Timothy D., D. Lisle, J. Schooler, S.D. Hodges, K.J. Klaaren, and S.J. LaFleur. 1993. Introspecting about reasons can reduce post-choice satisfaction. *Personality and Social Psychology Bulletin*, 19: 331-339.

Wilson, Timothy D. 2002. *Strangers to Ourselves*. Cambridge, MA: Harvard University Press.

Worchel, Stephen, Jerry Lee, and Akanbi Adewole. 1975. Effects of supply and demand on ratings of object value. *Journal of Personality and Social Psychology*. Vol 32(5), 906-914.

Index

loss *versus* win situations, 99–101
mid brain, 3, 7
    working with old and new brains, 101–102
reading/listening to stories, 114
SCR (skin conductance response), 103
environment assessment, old brain, 3, 69–70, 116
Epinions.com, 124, 125
event boundaries, storytelling, 113
event structure perception, storytelling, 113–114

F

Facebook.com, 127
    invitations, 129–131
    persuasive communication, 132
    technological advancements since printing press, 122–123
Fear of Losing principle, 107
    privacy, 108
    security, 109
    word selection, 108
fMRI (functional Magnetic Resonance Imaging)
    decision making analysis, 56
    storytelling
        event structure perception, 113
        listening to/reading stories, 114
Fogg, B.J., 131
food
    and self-focus, 66–67, 68
    and sizing up people, 88–89
functional Magnetic Resonance Imaging (fMRI)
    decision making analysis, 56
    storytelling
        event structure perception, 113
        listening to/reading stories, 114

G–K

Gershon, Nahum, 112

hippocampus, 103
humans, *versus* animals, 4–6

impulse buying, mid brain, 3
Internet
    future, 132
    origin, 123–124
    today
        mass interpersonal communication, 128–130
        MIP (Mass Interpersonal Persuasion), 131
        persuasive communication, 132
        social networking, 124–128
invitations, 128–130

L

language processing
    new brain, 3
    reading/listening to stories, 114
Leakey, Richard, 30
Licklider, J.C.R., 123–124
Linkedin.com, 124, 126
losing
    decision making process, 100–101, 105–107
    Fear of Losing principle, 107
        privacy, 108
        security, 109
        word selection, 108

M

Mass Interpersonal Persuasion (MIP), 131
mid brain, 3
    amygdala, 6–7, 12

NOTES

NOTES

NOTES

NOTES

NOTES